THE SCREENWRITER'S
TROUBLESHOOTER

THE SCREENWRITER'S TROUBLESHOOTER

The Most Common Screenwriting Problems and How to Solve Them
With the Story-Type Method® Volume 2
By Emmanuel Oberg

Screenplay Unlimited, The Story-Type Method and The Structurator are registered trademarks of Screenplay Unlimited Ltd.

ISBN: 978-0-9954981-3-6 (e-book), 978-0-9954981-4-3 (paperback), 978-0-9954981-5-0 (hardcover with colour interior), 978-0-9954981–6-7 (hardcover with B&W interior)

By the same author in the Story-Type Method Series
Volume 1: *Screenwriting Unchained*
Volume 3: *Writing a Successful TV Series*

See If You Want to Find Out More... at the end of this book to access free content and receive a discount on our online courses

The Story-Type Method® Series Editor: Naomi Telford
Author photograph by Barbara Leatham Photography
Cover by JD Smith Design

The Screenwriter's Troubleshooter by Emmanuel Oberg – 1ˢᵗ ed.
Published in Great Britain in 2019 by

SCREENPLAY
Unlimited
PUBLISHING

10, Orange Street, Haymarket London WC2H 7DQ United Kingdom
Read more at www.screenplayunlimited.com

Emmanuel Oberg

THE SCREENWRITER'S

TROUBLESHOOTER

The Most Common
Screenwriting Problems
and How to Solve Them

 With The STORY-TYPE METHOD

Contents

"*Remember: When people tell you something's wrong or doesn't work for them, they are almost always right. When they tell you exactly what they think is wrong and how to fix it, they are almost always wrong.*"

—Neil Gaiman

"*I suppose it is tempting, if the only tool you have is a hammer, to treat everything as if it were a nail.*"

—Abraham Maslow

Introduction

I've spent more than two decades working in the film and TV industry. Most recently, writing feature films or TV series as a professional screenwriter for major studios, TV channels and independent producers. Before that, I analysed thousands of scripts, first as a reader, then as a script consultant and development executive.

Over the years, the many stories I've come across, while different on the surface, often exhibited similar issues underneath. I've written *The Screenwriter's Troubleshooter* to identify these common screenwriting problems and suggest practical steps to resolve them.

Of course, there is always more than one way to tackle a creative problem, but understanding its root is usually a key step towards a solution. Unfortunately, that's easier said than done.

Getting feedback helps, but writers often feel as though they could do with an interpreter to translate some of the comments they receive into actionable steps.

Without going into the farcical "make it funnier", development notes usually make sense – after all, they tend to be written by intelligent, experienced people – but they don't always indicate a clear path to a rewrite for a screenwriter. They often come across as too generic, too dogmatic or too cryptic, especially for those at the start of their career, who might not yet be used to filtering and processing them. Great notes are non-prescriptive yet immediately applicable. Not so great notes can still be useful, but they do require extra work.

Writers might well agree that their screenplay isn't working, but if feedback leaves them unsure as to what the problems are, it's going to be a struggle to get to a better draft.

Often, this situation stems from a confusion between symptoms and problems. For instance, readers point out a problem towards the end of a screenplay, but the ending not working is actually just the symptom of a structural problem – related to character, plot or theme – rooted far deeper in the story. The problem might manifest itself more clearly towards the end of the script, but it doesn't mean that it can be fixed simply by tweaking the last ten pages.

Trying to fix symptoms is likely to introduce a whole new set of problems and produce a script that's *different*, but not *better*. In the example above, you might come up with twenty different endings, but until you solve the actual problem underneath, you've not made progress. In some cases, you might even have taken a step backwards.

So let's try to get beyond the symptom, to the problem!

Here is how this book works:

The title of each section lists a symptom, as it might appear in notes sent by a producer, story editor, reader, financier or development exec. These symptoms are so common that many of them have become clichés. The first step in each section will be to go beyond the symptom and define the possible story problem(s) that might cause this symptom.

This "symptom to problem" translator benefits both sides:

If you're on the receiving end of these notes, hopefully this approach will help you to address them. Addressing notes doesn't mean implementing all the suggested solutions. It means identifying and resolving the problems in order to deliver a better draft, not just a different one. A development process is healthy when each draft builds on the strengths of the previous one and gradually reduces the number and severity of the problems.

If you're the sending party, this book might help you to go one step further in articulating what you perceive as being an issue. If you can be more specific about the problems you detect, focusing on asking the right questions and refraining from offering your own solutions, you'll make it easier for writers to understand what the actual problems are.

Once we've translated the symptom into potential problems or root causes, the second part of each section explores ways to address each note and keep these problems at bay.

Sounds good? Welcome on board!

Before we set off though, let's quickly discuss how you can make the most of this book.

How to Use This Book

In this book, we'll be using the Story-Type Method to look at the most common screenwriting problems and solutions for fixing them.

If you aren't familiar with this new approach to screenwriting, I recommend that you read the first book in the series, *Screenwriting Unchained*. Of course, I understand that you might not want to splurge on another volume if you've just bought this one, so you'll find a link to download a free sampler (first fifty pages) at the end of this book in If You Want to Find Out More... This sampler includes the introduction and most of the first chapter, providing an overview of the method, with many info-graphs and examples.

Although I'll try to briefly define some of the concepts detailed in *Screenwriting Unchained*, I will inevitably use terms that you might not be familiar with if you haven't read the first volume. To help overcome this hurdle, I've added a Story-Type Method Glossary at the end of this book, with definitions of the most important concepts, as well as links to chapters where they are discussed in more detail.

I wrote *Screenwriting Unchained* because I wanted to introduce a more flexible, less dogmatic approach to screenwriting. I took the time to discuss theoretical content and use detailed case studies to illustrate my method, each chapter, each section building on the previous one. This meant that it made more sense if read from cover to cover.

Where *Screenwriting Unchained* was strategic, *The Screenwriter's Troubleshooter* is tactical. Shorter, with independent sections, it's a practical handbook designed to help writers address specific development notes or problems they've identified in their screenplays. It's short on theory and focuses instead on easy-to-understand, fluff-free, actionable advice.

I've written this book as a reference guide, so that you can dive in at any point and read its sections in any order. I often draw examples from the same films, usually from case studies in *Screenwriting Unchained*. This means that reading the book from cover to cover will inevitably lead to some repetitions. In any given section, I won't assume you've read those preceding it, those related to it, or even the first volume in the series. I can live with these repetitions as long as you understand why they are there.

Sometimes, you don't want to spend years in therapy to solve a problem. You're deep in it and you want a way out, fast. This is what this book offers: direct access to essential information about the most common screenwriting problems that will hopefully get you on the way to solving issues before a looming deadline. An emergency toolkit to survive the script development process.

However, as with therapy, once you've addressed the crisis, to fully resolve the problem you might have to go deeper and explore dark corners you'd rather not disturb. While each section should provide enough information on its own to set you on the right path, you might need to dig further to solve the issue or prevent it from reoccurring. Yep, that means *less* writing short term, but it might also lead to *better* writing long term.

Therefore, at the end of each section, I'll mention:

- Connected problems discussed in this book. These references will be underlined.
- Sections of *Screenwriting Unchained* where you can find in-depth explanations, further guidance or examples / case studies related to the problem at hand.
- Sections of 12 Ways to a Stronger Screenplay – the rewrite guide in *Screenwriting Unchained* – that might cover the problem you're looking to solve.

One last thing... Although I'll often mention the three main story-types (plot-led, character-led and theme-led) defined in *Screenwriting Unchained*, I won't delve too much into hybrids and exceptions in this book. This doesn't mean that the problems or solutions provided only relate to the main story-types. It's just that developing a hybrid or an exception is like going off-piste: 1) you should know what you're doing, so experience and talent is key and 2) you're more or less on your own if something goes wrong!

So if you think you might be developing a hybrid or an exception, I recommend reading *Screenwriting Unchained* first – especially the Developing Something Else chapter – before looking into *The Screenwriter's Troubleshooter* for a solution to your problems. This should help with the "knowing what you're doing" part, and if you still find yourself in a high-risk zone, this book is more likely to provide the "not entirely on your own" part.

Right. Enough preamble. Time to embark on our troubleshooting quest!

The Most Common Screenwriting Problems

01 We Don't Care About the Protagonist

I had to start with this because it's by far the most common development note. The over-the-counter solution to this problem is to make the protagonist nicer, more sympathetic. For example, show the protagonist doing something good – like saving a cat – which suggests they can't be entirely bad. This is often the *worst* possible way to deal with this problem because a protagonist's conceptual "niceness" has little to do with what makes us care about them.

In a screenplay, we're not after *conceptual* identification (liking the protagonist, as in having sympathy for them or approving of what they are trying to achieve), but rather *emotional* identification (understanding the protagonist, as in feeling empathy, even if we disapprove of who they are or what they are trying to do).

In fact, if the point of a particular story is to have an unsympathetic protagonist, then asking the writer to "make the protagonist nicer" hurts the story and goes against the creative intent. In this kind of story where the whole narrative is about the evolution of a conceptually negative character (or failure to evolve if it has a tragic ending), making such a suggestion is likely to alienate the writer and prevent any genuine improvement to the story.

Before we address this note, let's define the term protagonist. A protagonist isn't simply the nicest character: Melvin Uddall in *As Good As it Gets* or Gru in *Despicable Me* don't fit that description. Neither is a protagonist the character who has the most screen time or the person whose life story we're exploring: Mozart has more screen time than Salieri in *Amadeus*. It also isn't the character who changes most, despite many screenwriting gurus insisting on that: In *Billy Elliot*, it's the antagonistic father who changes the most, not the protagonist. It's not always the point-of-view character: *The Hand That Rocks the Cradle* tells the story primarily from the point of view of the antagonist, which makes it a fascinating exception. So what is a protagonist?

Protagonist comes from the Greek word *protagonistes*, which means *the one who fights in the front row*. This suggests the character who is the most likely to get hurt or killed during the battle. This powerful image leads us to the actual definition of a protagonist: the character – or group of characters sharing the same goal – who experiences the most conflict in the story. Let's repeat for clarity: not the nicest, the most important, the most well-known, the most active, the point-of-view character or the character who changes most. Just the character who experiences the most conflict.

This is crucial because it's this conflict that helps us to identify emotionally with that character, hence care about them.

So, what should we be focusing on?

1) Check that the protagonist experiences enough conflict.

This can be an issue in some **plot-led stories** (where the main problem lies outside the protagonist). For example, in a superhero or action movie where the protagonist has so many powers or skills that they experience little conflict despite all the fights and set pieces. Conflict comes from the difference in strength between the protagonist and the obstacles. The stronger the protagonist, the more you need to work on the obstacles / antagonist. This is what made the original *Bourne Trilogy* so successful: giving a strong protagonist an equally strong internal conflict (Bourne's amnesia) as well as competent, resourceful, determined antagonists.

The more negative the protagonist is, conceptually or morally, the more conflict they need to experience in order to override the audience's conceptual lack of sympathy. A protagonist who has primarily negative character traits at the start of a story usually needs to experience a lot of conflict if we want the audience to empathise with them.

This need for conflict is even stronger in a **character-led story**, where the main problem is internal and the audience gives the protagonist the unconscious need to change. For example, in

Groundhog Day, Phil Connors has to live the worst day of his life repeatedly, which means *a lot* of conflict for him.

2) The audience needs to feel that someone can do something about the main problem in the story. The protagonist might *want* to achieve something consciously, as in a **plot-led story**, or to fulfil an unconscious *need*, as in a **character-led story**, but it has to be possible for *someone* to do *something* about a main problem. *Drama*, in Greek, means action. Without a dramatic action or evolution, there is no drama.

So the audience should be able to figure out, fairly early in the story, consciously or not, who *wants* or *needs* what and why, as this defines the main problem. But they also need to understand what can be done about this problem. In other words, the audience needs to feel that the protagonist stands a chance of succeeding, even if they fear they might fail. Striking the right balance between hope and fear in the audience as the story progresses is key.

It can be very alienating for an audience to watch a protagonist glide into self-destruction, or deal with a fatal disease with no hope of remission. If there is nothing the protagonist can do about a problem, there is no hope. So find another protagonist or co-protagonist who can do something about it. Provide an alternate emotional point of view, or find another way to tell the story. Otherwise, you might have pathos but pathos isn't drama. This is a common issue in poorly designed **character-led stories.** *Leaving Las Vegas* avoided this problem thanks to Sera's character, who introduced both an alternative emotional point of view and a dilemma for protagonist Ben Sanderson. In *The Intouchables*, Philippe's main problem isn't that he's disabled. There's nothing he can do about that. It's that he's lost his wife and has to learn to live without her. This is made very clear in the story, which allows us to hope for a positive outcome.

3) Sometimes the audience is unable to understand or relate to the conflict that a character faces if this conflict is too abstract or unusual.

The most efficient way to aid identification is to centre the film around a conflict that everyone can relate to. For example, an undeserved punishment is a classic way to get the audience to feel close to a character. This was exploited by Hitchcock in many of his thrillers, often based around a character accused of a murder we know they haven't committed. *The Fugitive* (both the original TV series and the movie) is another well-known example. The key, here, is that the audience has no doubt that the protagonist is innocent (because that warrants the "undeserved" part of the punishment). If you make it a mystery instead, as in *Gone Girl*, and we don't know whether the protagonist has committed a murder or not, you get an interesting exception based more on intellectual than emotional gratification. It might be a good way to avoid what could be seen as a cliché today, but it does take away the pure thriller element.

Another example of a universally relatable conflict is embarrassment, often used in comedy. The opening sequence of *There's Something About Mary*, especially the traumatic bathroom scene, provides a classical illustration. It's hard not to identify with Ted after his aborted prom night with Mary. This is because everyone can relate to such extreme embarrassment, which is, by the way, also an undeserved punishment (we know that he isn't a pervert and that he *was* looking at the doves!).

A last example to illustrate this notion of universal conflict: in *Amadeus*, Mozart's main conflict is that it's difficult to create, even when you're a genius. This conflict might resonate with creative people, but a wider audience might find it fairly abstract. So the story is cleverly centred around Salieri instead, whose main source of conflict is his jealousy. This is a much more universal conflict and it makes Salieri a better protagonist for that reason: even if we're fascinated by Mozart, the main character, it's much easier to relate to Salieri, especially in the first half of the film.

4) A frequent issue in plot-led stories is that the audience doesn't care about the protagonist because the protagonist is flat. Yes, there is a clear goal, with many obstacles and lots of conflict, yet somehow the character fails to resonate. This is often because the protagonist has no journey, no growth, no inner conflict. Often we can tackle this by bringing in a character-led subplot, something within the protagonist that needs to change. In a plot-led story, this need for change should be less important than the main problem in the story (otherwise we'd have a character-led story!) but it should still define a clear evolution for the character. Provided that the conflict experienced through the story is causing this evolution, it should make us care more about the protagonist. Jack Walsh in *Midnight Run* illustrates this approach perfectly. The main problem is external (primarily mobster Serrano), but Walsh's internal need to change is explored through his conflictual relationship with catalyst character Mardukas and the dilemma it causes: Will Walsh do the right thing and let Mardukas go, or will he bring the fugitive back to collect the bounty? This is what makes the protagonist – and the story – more interesting. The audience cares about Walsh because thanks to this character arc and dilemma, he becomes a three-dimensional protagonist. More on this in 05 The Characters Are Flat, Two-Dimensional.

5) Sometimes, all of this is in place and yet the audience still struggles to care about the protagonist. **In this case we might need to look at the way we manage information in the story**. It's usually not a problem to know *more* than the protagonist for a while, especially if we exploit this knowledge as a dramatic irony (when the audience knows something that at least one character isn't aware of). For example, in *The Apartment*, protagonist C.C. Baxter doesn't know that his boss is dating Fran Kubelik, the woman Baxter loves. We do. Or in *Titanic*: Unlike all the characters in the film, we know from the beginning that this boat will sink! However, knowing *less* than the protagonist over a long period of time regarding important elements of the story often creates a distance between the protagonist and the audience. For example, the protagonist of a character-led story might know things about their past that they don't share with the audience. Or the protagonist of a plot-led story – say in a detective story – won't share their findings about the case. This might work in a novel, where readers enjoy the intellectual puzzle, but is likely to be less effective in a movie where a stronger emotional gratification is expected.

A film like *Cake* illustrates this potential problem very well. Despite Jennifer Aniston's fine performance, we need to find out more about Claire's backstory before we can relate to her and understand her conflict. It's only when we find out, rather late in the story, that she lost her son in a car accident, that we are able to identify with her and become more involved emotionally with her character. But for many in the audience, it might come too late. We spend the first half of the film unable to engage with Claire because she comes across as too distant, too cold, despite all the conflict she is clearly going through. We're kept at arms-length for too long, unable to understand her pain and unhappiness. This is because of the way information is managed in the film: We can't feel close to a character who hides crucial pieces of information from the audience over such a long period of time. It makes it too difficult for us to understand their actions, decisions and emotions.

David O. Russell found a better way to handle exposition (showing us what happened before the story began) in *Silver Linings Playbook*. By minute fifteen, we're told everything we need to learn about Pat's past. This means we can empathise and identify with him early on. We're on board from the start, and we care about him. Similarly, in *Three Billboards Outside Ebbing, Missouri*, we quickly learn what we need to know about Mildred Hayes. There is an element of mystery that hooks us in as the story starts, but we soon catch up with her. We can identify and empathise with Mildred because we understand her goal and motivation: she wants justice for her daughter who was raped and murdered. We care about Mildred not only because of the conflict she experiences, but also because of the information we are given early on.

So, if you want the audience to care about your protagonist, make sure they don't know less than the protagonist over a long period of time. Of course, we don't need to know the whole backstory of the character. This only refers to any element in the story that helps the audience understand the situation the protagonist faces, the decisions they make and the emotions they experience as they try to resolve the main problem in the story.

One way of preventing a mystery from getting in the way of an emotional identification can be as easy as making sure that the protagonist doesn't remember their past either and is trying to put the pieces back together – along with the audience – as the story unfolds. We call this a *cold start*. It's used in *The Bourne Identity*, *Cowboys & Aliens*, *Before I Go to Sleep*, *Predators* or *The Maze Runner*. Any story that gives the protagonist a *cold start* keeps the audience close to the character despite the mystery about their past because we look for information alongside them, instead of feeling alienated by knowledge they don't care to share with us. It's much more effective than shutting us out, especially if the missing information relates to the main plot. Managing conflict and managing information are two sides of the same coin. If we, as storytellers, neglect or mishandle either, we're likely to stand on shaky ground.

6) Often we don't care about the protagonist because we don't know enough about the character. Not what they might be hiding from us as in the point above, but who they are. This is often the case in **plot-led stories** with weak set-ups (first ten to fifteen minutes of the film). Throwing a protagonist into high-octane action before the audience has a chance to know them as a person might prevent us from caring about them even though they experience a lot of conflict. Successful action thrillers such as *Gravity* or *Jaws* take the time to introduce the characters before all hell breaks loose. We don't need half an hour to achieve this, but taking ten to fifteen minutes to introduce the characters so we get acquainted with them before they end up in trouble can pay huge dividends. If you're concerned this might lead to an overly long set-up, then consider using a teaser flashback: Start with a short, exciting sequence that sets the tone and genre while raising interesting questions using mystery or dramatic irony, then go back to introducing your characters, as in *John Wick* or *Breaking Bad*.

Taking the time to introduce your characters will also help with casting because a three-dimensional character will be far easier to cast. Good actors want to have something to defend in a part. So if you need a cast to get your project off the ground, make sure you have well-rounded characters. If you think this might be an issue in your project, re-working the set-up is usually a good place to start.

7) If the protagonist is a "bad guy" conceptually or morally (say, a criminal) then creating worse characters that make the protagonist look good in contrast might help. For example, in *Heat*, bank robber Neil McCauley could be perceived as a fairly negative protagonist, but we have Waingro and Van Zant who are conceptually worse than him. They make McCauley look like a pretty good guy in comparison. Detective Vincent Hanna is the antagonist (not a negative character, just a character whose goal is in direct opposition to the protagonist's goal, and the main source of conflict). Waingro and Van Zant are villains. They are morally wrong, therefore conceptually worse than the protagonist and antagonist, which allows us to empathise and identify with both McCauley and Hannah. McCauley doesn't have to save a cat or do something conceptually nice for us to care about him, thanks to Waingro and Van Zant.

Solutions

To sum this up, when this note lands on your desk, here is a suggested checklist:

✓ **Does the protagonist experience enough conflict?** Whether they are everyday people (Mildred Hayes in *Three Billboards Outside Ebbing, Missouri*, C.C. Baxter in *The Apartment*), extraordinary characters or superheroes (Jason Bourne, Diana in *Wonder Woman*), villains (Gru in *Despicable Me*, Maleficent), criminals (McCauley in *Heat*), underdogs (Rocky Balboa in *Rocky*) or depressive losers (Ben Sanderson in *Leaving Las Vegas*), audiences will identify emotionally with a character if they experience more conflict than the other characters in the story, and if they can relate to this conflict. Make sure you strike the right balance between the strength of the protagonist and the strength of the obstacles they face. A protagonist has to face obstacles that are strong *for them* in order to generate a true sense of conflict and help identification.

✓ **Can *someone* do *something* about the main problem in the story?** If nothing can be done, you might have pathos but not drama, and the audience will not care about the protagonist. So make sure that you strike the right balance between the hope that the audience has for the protagonist to succeed, and the fear that they might fail.

✓ **Can the audience understand and relate to the conflict experienced by your protagonist?** Feeling sorry conceptually for someone doesn't mean that we'll be able to identify with them emotionally. If the main source of conflict in your story is too abstract or if it's something that the majority of the audience is unlikely to have experienced, try to find universal sources of conflict that anyone can relate to (undeserved punishment, embarrassment, jealousy etc).

✓ **Is your protagonist flat?** Do you need an evolution (of the protagonist, of the relationship between two characters) or a dilemma to add emotional depth and make the story more interesting?

✓ **Does the protagonist know something about their past that they don't share with the audience?** This can be alienating and can prevent your audience from identifying with the protagonist. Consider using a *cold start* so that if we don't know something important about the protagonist's past, they don't know it either.

✓ **Do we know enough about the protagonist to care about the outcome?** Did you take the time to introduce the characters so that we feel we know them before all hell breaks loose?

✓ **If the protagonist is morally or conceptually negative, would creating "worse" characters help to make the protagonist look good in contrast?** This can help in gangster movies (*The Godfather, Heat*) or revenge stories (*John Wick*).

Of course, much of this only applies if there is a clear protagonist in the story. This isn't always the case, for example in **theme-led stories** (multi-stranded narratives where the main problem usually lies in society) and in many hybrids and exceptions. We'll explore this further in 18 There Is No Clear Protagonist, which is another common note (often describing a symptom rather than a problem).

Connected Problems in This Book

- 02 We Don't Care About the Story
- 05 The Characters Are Flat, Two-Dimensional
- 06 The Character Logic Is Fuzzy
- 14 The Characters' Backstories Are Irrelevant / Pointless
- 13 The Characters Are Stereotypes or Clichés
- 20 The Conflict Is Artificial or Inconsequential
- 18 There Is No Clear Protagonist
- 28 The Protagonist Is Not Strong Enough

Sections in Screenwriting Unchained

- 1.3 Is Maslow Running the Show?

- 'Managing Conflict' and 'Managing Information' in 2.1 Behind the Scenes
- 'Choosing the Best Protagonist' in 2.2 Sequence the Action
- 'Story World', 'A Good Set-Up', 'Characterisation', 'Protagonist vs Antagonist', 'Protagonist vs Main Character', 'Hero vs Protagonist', 'Cold Start' and 'Flashbacks: To FB or Not to FB' in 2.3 Craft the Draft

Sections in 12 Ways to a Stronger Screenplay

- M-Factor (What's at Stake?)
- Set-up / Story World
- Managing Conflict (Who Wants / Needs What and Why?)
- Managing Information (Who Knows What When?)
- Character (Change, Growth or Steadfast?)
- Antagonist or Catalyst: Who Is Testing Your Protagonist?

02 We Don't Care About the Story

Ouch. This one hurts even more than the first one.

How could someone *not* care about our story when we thought we had ticked all the boxes?

Clear protagonist: check. We understand the goal (conscious want or unconscious need) of the protagonist: check. Strong obstacles in the way and lots of conflict: check. The protagonist needs to grow or change: check. And yet, we have little interest in finding out how the story will unfold and how it will end. We just don't care about the story.

Let's look at the most common reasons for this note to pop up

1) The story has no meaning. There is no theme, which is what the story is about. So the audience understands who wants or needs what and why, but it doesn't matter because the story has no relevance.

This is often the case in plot-led stories (where the main problem lies outside of the protagonist). Even an action film or a sci-fi should be about something relevant to a contemporary audience. The meaning of the story doesn't have to be philosophical, political or spiritual, but there should be some emotional truth in the story. For example, in *Gravity*, the plot is about survival, but the theme is about resilience and re-birth. We care about the story, about the survival of the characters, partly because the story explores that theme.

Although less likely, a weak theme can also compromise character-led stories (where the main problem lies within the protagonist). We get the angst of the central character. We understand that they are depressed or suicidal, but we don't see the point of the story, because the issue isn't relevant to us. Instead of feeling sorry for the protagonist, we feel sorry for ourselves and can't see the end of the film soon enough. Checking that the main dramatic evolution in a character-led story is linked to a strong theme might help with this.

Or you might be developing a theme-led story, a multi-stranded narrative where the main problem usually lies in society. The theme might not be clear enough or the strands might not all be connected to the same theme, so the audience struggles to understand what the story is about. Or the audience doesn't care about that specific problem in society, because we don't feel it concerns us, or it doesn't suggest a conflictual or interesting issue.

2) Another possibility, especially in some action movies, is that we might not care about the story because we don't care about the characters. Structure isn't only about plot.

So if it sounds like this could be a problem in your story, look at the characters. Do we understand them even if we don't approve of them or their actions? Did you take the time to introduce them before getting them hit by that volcano / twister / tsunami / asteroid / bunch of terrorists / serial killer? If they are complex characters in a character-led story, can someone – themselves or other characters – do something about their problem, consciously or not, or is it only about them suffering? Because in that case, the audience will suffer too, but not in a good way. This relates to the previous problem, 01 We Don't Care About the Protagonist.

3) Most of the time though, this note shows up because we don't understand what's at stake: What happens if the protagonist fails to reach a conscious goal in a plot-led story, or an unconscious need to change in a character-led story. Or, if we do understand the stakes, we don't care because they are not high enough. In a theme-led story, there is rarely one thing at stake overall as the main problem tends to lie in society and often can't be solved. This is why it's crucial in these instances to structure and develop each strand properly and make sure your audience cares about what's at stake in each strand. If your story is multi-stranded, the suggestions below might not apply to the whole story but they are likely to apply to most of the strands.

"What's at stake?" is the question most often asked by executives and producers when they don't care about the story or when the stakes are not high enough. What they mean is: "Why should we want to know what's going to happen next?" A story that fails to clarify this early on starts with a strong handicap.

To sum it up, the three main reasons why we might not care about the story are because the story has a weak theme, because we don't care about the characters or because what's at stake isn't clear or the stakes aren't high enough.

Solutions

So how do we address this note?

✓ **Make sure your story has something to say.** Define a clear theme (What is the story about?) and explore it throughout the story, if not through the main plot, at least through one of the subplots. It doesn't have to be a philosophical "message", it can be a truthful evolution, a question about society or an emotional journey.

✓ **Check that we care about your characters.** Story structure is a combination of plot, character and theme. If we don't care about your characters – especially about your protagonist, when there is one – it's going to be difficult to care about the story, no matter how many set pieces or how much CGI you throw at the screen. You can find more on this in 01 We Don't Care About the Protagonist and 24 There Is No Clear Antagonist.

✓ **Find a compelling answer to the question: What will happen if the protagonist fails to solve the main problem?** This is how you'll identify what's at stake in the story. Make sure this defines something that makes us feel sad, anxious or terrified, or any negative feeling you can come up with. It should be something we don't want to see happen to the characters. For example, in *Silver Linings Playbook*, if Pat doesn't change, he will go back to jail or to the hospital and he won't get to spend the rest of his life with Tiffany. In *Gravity* or *Misery*, the protagonist's life is at stake.

✓ **If thinking of the protagonist's possible failure brings a neutral or positive feeling**, you either have a structural problem or the actual story structure isn't about what the character *wants* (plot-led side) but what the character *needs* (character-led side). In that case, the character needs to realise they are wrong to pursue their conscious goal. Giving it up means success. This is what's really at stake in the story.

For example, *Little Miss Sunshine* is a character-led story disguised as plot-led, just like *Two Days, One Night* or *Silver Linings Playbook*. It looks likes the goal, what's at stake, is to get Olive to the beauty contest on time (or for Sandra to get her job back, or for Pat to get back with his estranged wife). However, what's really at stake in the story is for the family to be less dysfunctional (or for Sandra to get her self-esteem back, or for Pat to move on and get better). You need to define this clearly, as well as what will happen – the negative consequences – if the change doesn't take place and deal with it accordingly. Otherwise it's unlikely your story will ever fire on all cylinders.

✓ **Identify where the main problem sits in Maslow's Hierarchy of Needs**, as this will help to determine whether the stakes are high enough or need to be raised, either from the start or as the story unfolds. This requires more time to explain, but it's at the core of what I call the M-Factor (short for Maslow factor), a key element in assessing the potential audience of a story and its universality. You can find out more about this in the first chapter of *Screenwriting Unchained*.

Let's look at *Two Days, One Night* briefly. While the story is really about the protagonist getting her self-esteem back, we are drawn in further by a concern for her safety. If Sandra doesn't get her job back, she loses her house. When her depression leads her to contemplate suicide, the story becomes about survival. While not everyone sees self-esteem as a high-level concern, a larger potential audience can relate to safety and survival. This considerably raises the stakes and opens the story to a significantly wider audience.

✓   **Consider using a time-lock to increase the tension.** If the protagonist only has a limited amount of time to reach the goal / change, this might help the audience to get more involved in the story. Having this time-lock in the title itself, as in *Two Days, One Night* or *48 Hours*, helps even further when pitching the project.

✓   Finally, it's often a good idea **to raise the stakes as the story unfolds.** We might start with saving the protagonist's life and then realise that their family or the wider community is at risk too. Or we could first understand that the protagonist will be unhappy if they don't fulfil their need to change, but then realise that they might commit suicide if they fail. All this can help increase or renew interest in the story because it raises the stakes and strengthens the dramatic question (Will the protagonist reach the goal?).

Connected Problems in This Book
* 01 We Don't Care About the Protagonist
* 03 The Story Takes Too Long to Start
* 04 The Story Is Linear, Feels Predictable
* 08 The Story Is Confusing
* 09 The Screenplay Is Too Dry or Not Visual Enough
* 11 The Screenplay Is Written Like a Novel
* 39 The Theme Overshadows the Story
* 25 The Narrative Is Episodic or Repetitive
* 40 The Premise Is an Artificial Excuse For Action
* 16 The Scenes Are Aimless, There Is No Dramatic Conflict
* 19 The Script Feels Formulaic
* 35 The Script Is Unnecessarily Complex

Sections in Screenwriting Unchained
* 1.1 What's Wrong with the Three-Act Structure?
* 1.2 So What Do We Need to Get It Right?
* 1.3 Is Maslow Running the Show?
* 'Managing Conflict' and 'Managing Information' in 2.1 Behind the Scenes.

- 2.2 Sequence the Action
- 3.2 Sequence the Evolution
- 4.2 Sequence the Strands
- 'Genre', 'A Good Set-Up', 'Story World', 'Characterisation', 'Theme', 'Inciting Incident vs Inciting Action' and 'Time-Locks' in 2.3 Craft the Draft

Sections in 12 Ways to a Stronger Screenplay

- Story-Type and Genre
- M-Factor (What's at Stake?)
- Theme (What Is the Story About?)
- Set-up / Story World
- Managing Conflict (Who Wants / Needs What and Why?)
- Managing Information (Who Knows What When?)
- Character (Change, Growth or Steadfast?)
- Antagonist or Catalyst? Who Is Testing Your Protagonist?
- Time-Lock

03 The Story Takes Too Long to Start

The logistical three-act structure and its 30-60-30 paradigm (or 25-50-25 nowadays) is largely to blame for this complaint. It's easy to read these superficial theories about story structure and believe that we have until minute twenty-five or thirty to get the story started. This is a fundamental flaw in many scripts. In this age of short attention spans, you have ten, possibly fifteen minutes to grab the reader's or the audience's attention. That means ten to fifteen pages in a conventionally formatted script (what we call the set-up). In most cases, this means that we need to know who wants or needs what and why as soon as possible.

This doesn't mean that we can't take the time to introduce the characters so that we care about them by the time the dramatic action kicks in, or to set up the story world so that we understand the context of the story. But taking thirty minutes – or even twenty-five – to achieve this is simply too long. Ideally, we should know what's at stake – or, in a theme-led story, what the movie is about – by minute fifteen.

If that's not possible, you could start the story with an exciting action sequence – preferably related to the main plot – as in most instalments of *Indiana Jones*, *James Bond* or *Mission Impossible*; with a teaser flashback so that we get a sense of what's to come as in *John Wick*, *Goodfellas* or *Run All Night*; or with a *Cold Start* that hooks us with a mystery and gives us something to investigate alongside the protagonist, as in *The Bourne Identity*, *Predators*, *The Maze Runner* or *Before I Go to Sleep*.

The solution to this problem often lies in managing information, which means focusing on the "Who knows what when?" side of story structure, using tools such as mystery, surprise, dramatic irony and suspense. For example, you could use dramatic irony to tell the audience something the protagonist doesn't know, as in *The Truman Show* (Truman doesn't know he's the central character of a TV show). This is what the teaser flashback achieves in *The Hangover* (the protagonists don't know that their stag night is going to end badly). Or something that every one in the audience knows even before the film starts, but the protagonist doesn't, as in *Titanic* (that boat is going to sink) or *Misery* (Nurse Annie is a nutter). This leads us to experience conflict for the protagonist and raises an interesting ironic question right away: When and how will the protagonist find out? So even if the protagonist doesn't have a strong goal from the get go, we lend an unconscious goal to the protagonist, which is to find out what we know and they don't.

In almost all disaster movies – where it takes time to set up all the characters before disaster strikes – we have that shot showing the lava slowly rising inside the volcano, or the fire starting in an empty room in the soon-to-be towering inferno, or mission control mentioning a distant cloud of satellite debris. This is dramatic irony. It gives us a taste of the conflict to come, a hint that things are going to get worse soon – hence the situation will be more exciting – so that we don't leave the theatre, close the script, fall asleep or switch channels while the characters and story world are set up.

Solutions

Here is what we can do to get the story started quickly:

✓   **Make sure that by page fifteen, you have started the main dramatic action or evolution** (we're already in dramatic Act 2 of a **plot-led** or **character-led story**) as in *Jaws, Midnight Run, Silver Linings Playbook* or *Two Days, One Night.* Or check you've set up the theme and the main action / evolution in at least one of the strands in a **theme-led story,** preferably more than one to suggest that we're following an unconventionally structured story, as in *Crash, Dunkirk* or *Cloud Atlas.*

✓   If that's not possible, you might need an inciting action (a dramatic sequence in Act 1) rather than an isolated inciting incident. **Make sure you're managing conflict and information effectively in dramatic Act 1 in order to** create some other form of suspense. For example, you could consider using dramatic irony as in *Misery*: Tell the audience that the protagonist is in trouble and keep the protagonist unaware. The audience will give the protagonist the unconscious goal of realising this, and thus can tolerate a longer first dramatic act (before the main dramatic action or evolution starts).

✓ **Consider using a mystery to hook the audience with a Cold Start**, as in *The Maze Runner, Before I Go to Sleep, Cowboys & Aliens, Predators* or *Bourne Identity*. This will allow you to raise an interesting intellectual question without alienating the audience by having a protagonist who knows more than they do over a long period of time. In this instance, the audience knows as little as the protagonist, so we can identify with the character while they try to solve the mystery.

✓ **Consider crafting an action sequence or a teaser flashback to give the audience something exciting before you start the actual set-up.** Often, this action sequence or teaser flashback will set up some form of mystery or dramatic irony: the audience will know that things are soon going to get worse, or we'll want to know how the protagonist will get into that situation, and how they'll find a way out of it. This is what happens in *John Wick, Breaking Bad, Goodfellas, The Hangover* or *Run All Night*.

Connected Problems in This Book

- 01 We Don't Care About the Protagonist
- 02 We Don't Care About the Story
- 08 The Story Is Confusing
- 35 The Script Is Unnecessarily Complex

Sections in Screenwriting Unchained

- 1.1 What's Wrong with the Three-Act Structure?
- 1.2 So What Do We Need to Get It Right?
- 1.3 Is Maslow Running the Show?

- 'Managing Conflict' and 'Managing Information' in 2.1 Behind the Scenes
- 'Genre', 'A Good Set-Up', 'Story World', 'Inciting Incident vs Inciting Action', 'Flashbacks: To FB or not to FB?' and 'Cold Start' in 2.3 Craft the Draft

Sections in 12 Ways to a Stronger Screenplay

- Story-Type and Genre
- M-Factor (What's At Stake?)
- Theme (What Is the Story About?)
- Set-up / Story World
- Managing Conflict (Who Wants / Needs What and Why?)
- Managing Information (Who Knows What When?)

04 The Story Is Linear, Feels Predictable

A story feels predictable when it tells us where we're going, and gets us there in a straight line or allows us to predict the outcome. We want to know where we're heading, but we want to be surprised on the way. Also, we shouldn't be in a position where we can figure out whether the protagonist will succeed or fail before the end.

Getting this note often comes down to one of two reasons

1) The audience is able to answer the dramatic question (Will the protagonist reach the goal?) too early. This can be because it feels too easy, so we guess the protagonist is likely to succeed. Or the opposite: it feels too difficult, so we expect the protagonist to fail. Either way, if we can answer the dramatic question too early, we lose interest as the outcome of the story becomes predictable.

In this case, we need to find a better balance between the strength of the protagonist and the strength of the obstacles. The obstacles need to be high enough to generate conflict, but not so high that the protagonist can't overcome them. You can either vary the strength of the obstacles, or the strength of the protagonist, or both. To take a trivial example, because Superman is so strong, we need Kryptonite to weaken him. Paul Sheldon is badly wounded after a car accident in *Misery*, so that simple actions such as stepping out of a wheelchair become a huge effort. More importantly, we won't question why he can't simply overpower Nurse Annie. He is physically disabled and she's a very strong woman (we see that she's able to carry him out of the car wreck at the beginning). If you don't get the balance of power right between the protagonist and the obstacles (or antagonist when there is one), the story becomes artificial or overly predictable.

Using the fractal aspect of story structure – designing strong dramatic sequences – and raising the stakes during the story can also help to strengthen the dramatic question and renew the audience's interest. More on this later.

2) We're not managing information efficiently. This means we're not focusing on the "Who knows what when?" side of story structure, which is just as important as the "Who wants or needs what and why?" side. Perhaps we need more surprises to change the plot's direction, or we should vary the tools we use. When the protagonist has a plan, it shouldn't go as expected. That's boring. Once the audience understands what the protagonist wants or needs, which defines the destination of the story, we should still be surprised with the way they get there. In other words, the main dramatic action or evolution in the story should never follow a straight line. The key here is for the writer to use all the tools at their disposal regarding managing information: mystery, surprise, dramatic irony and suspense.

Inexperienced writers sometimes resist sharing information with the audience. They have a tendency to overuse mystery to privilege a final revelation, which is often wasted because the reader loses interest and moves on to the next script or the audience has walked out of the film before it reaches that point.

Writers with a literary background, whether they are experienced or not, might make the same mistake simply because the exclusive use of mystery over a long period of time tends to work well in a novel. In that medium, the process can be more intellectual than emotional, yet still be rewarding for the reader. This is how a "whodunit" or a murder mystery is designed. Although it works well in novels, and can even work well in a script if it's read like a novel, mystery on its own tends to fall flat once translated onto the screen.

Instead of relying on mystery over most of the film to come up with a big surprise at the end, consider giving the audience more information early on. This could be done using a surprise, keeping some of the characters in the dark about it, and then exploiting this information as a dramatic irony (the audience knows something that at least one character is unaware of). This happens in *Gone*

Girl, where the main mystery is resolved around the middle of the film as a surprise and is then exploited as a dramatic irony.

Or, if you do sustain a long mystery, make sure you also use surprise, suspense and dramatic irony to make the journey less linear and more exciting. This is what successful adaptations of modern whodunits achieve. For example, *The Girl on the Train* keeps the main mystery almost until the end of the story, but mixes it with dramatic irony and surprises along the way.

Solutions

If you're told that your story is predictable or too linear, focus on the following areas:

✓ **Verify you're balancing the strength of the obstacles with the strength of your protagonist in order to keep the dramatic question alive.** If the protagonist evolves, it usually means that the obstacles have to evolve as well so that the story doesn't become too easy to figure out.

✓ **Check that you're managing information in a varied, exciting and effective way**, relying on all the tools available (mystery, surprise, dramatic irony and suspense) and not just on one or two (usually mystery and a final surprise).

✓ If you're dealing with a **plot-led story, make sure you break down your main dramatic action into dramatic sequences,** using subgoals (ways for the protagonist to reach the goal). If you're dealing with a **character-led story, try to map the change and sequence the evolution of the protagonist** so that the conflict generated from the protagonist's dramatic action forces the character to change, one emotional / psychological step at a time. If you're designing a **theme-led story, verify that all the strands are connected to the same theme**, and that as many strands as possible are structured as plot-led or character-led so the audience knows what's at stake in each strand. More on this in 07 The Story Sags in the Middle.

✓ **See if you can find a way to raise the stakes as the story unfolds,** so that what happens if the protagonist fails to reach the conscious goal / unconscious need becomes even less desirable, not only for the character(s) but for the audience. This can usually be achieved by introducing an unexpected obstacle, by revealing that an obstacle or antagonist is stronger than we thought, or that the threat to the character(s) or the story world is higher than expected.

Connected Problems in This Book

- 08 The Story Is Confusing
- 25 The Narrative Is Episodic or Repetitive
- 01 We Don't Care About the Protagonist
- 07 The Story Sags in the Middle

Sections in Screenwriting Unchained

- 1.1 What's Wrong with the Three-Act Structure?
- 1.3 Is Maslow Running the Show?
- 'Managing Conflict' and 'Managing Information' in 2.1 Behind the Scenes
- 2.2 Sequence the Action and 2.3 Craft the Draft
- 3.2 Sequence the Evolution and 3.3 Grow the Draft
- 4.2 Sequence the Strands and 4.3 Weave the Draft

Sections in 12 Ways to a Stronger Screenplay

- M-Factor (What's at Stake?)
- Fractal Aspect of Story Structure
- Managing Conflict (Who Wants / Needs What and Why?)
- Managing Information (Who Knows What When?)

05 The Characters Are Flat, Two-Dimensional

A flat, two-dimensional character is a one-note character, a cliché who is only one thing in the story: the jealous lover, the stupid blonde, the fearless hero, the racist cop, the vicious serial-killer... It's difficult to find such characters interesting or believable because human beings are more complex than that. So how do we address this?

The over-the-counter solution is often misguided. Whenever people see flat characters, the knee-jerk reaction is to suggest a "character arc": give the character a flaw to generate internal conflict and bring about change. This dogma comes from one of the biggest misconceptions in the business: the assumption that the protagonist is the character who changes most in the story.

First, let's correct this false assumption. **The protagonist isn't the character who changes most in the story,** at least not in all stories. As we'll see below, there are excellent stories where the protagonist doesn't change (the character is steadfast), and even some stories where there is no protagonist at all (for example multi-stranded narratives that we call theme-led stories). There is certainly a case where the protagonist is the character who changes most: in character-led stories, where the main problem lies within the protagonist and the protagonist needs to change in order to move on. But in every other story-type, the protagonist is not *necessarily* the character who changes most.

Then, let's look at the unnecessary dogma. Because of the above assumption, and because a contemporary audience needs more complex characters than those from the last century, most screenwriting gurus have started to make this "character arc" a requirement, even when there is no need for the protagonist to change and when it could go against the creative intent or the genre. This forces artificial change in every protagonist, even in an action film where frankly it's often not necessary and can even take away some of the fun or confuse the stakes during the climax. Ever since *Lethal Weapon* and *Die Hard* (both great films and huge commercial successes), we have the dead or estranged spouse, the failed marriage, the estranged children, etc. All these have become clichés. This trauma in the protagonist's backstory is used as a shortcut to create identification. This kind of conflict can help us to sympathise with a character, but that's certainly not the only way to give them depth, especially when the past trauma bears no relation to the main plot. Unless you're making fun of this cliché – as in *John Wick*, by killing the dog sent by the dead wife from beyond the grave – you may not be helping your story.

So if you get a note that your characters are flat, let's first look at how to deal with this when it applies to the protagonist, and then we'll see how we can deal with other characters.

As explained above, this need for a "character arc" in a protagonist isn't true for all stories. Even when there *is* an evolution, it can take different forms depending on the story-type of the project.

In **plot-led stories** – when the main problem lies outside the protagonist – there is no need for the protagonist to change because there is nothing wrong with them. For example, Chris Gardner in *The Pursuit of Happyness* doesn't change; he's a steadfast character. However, especially in modern movies, the protagonist usually grows, either as a result of the conflict experienced during the story, like Ripley in *Alien*, or as a condition to be able to reach the goal, as in *Billy Elliot*, where Billy has to stand up to his father in order to fulfil his aspiration to become a ballet dancer. Either way, this growth gives depth to the characters and makes them dynamic human beings rather than cardboard cut-outs.

However, in **character-led stories**, where the main problem lies within the protagonist – hence the protagonist *is* the antagonist – the character needs to change, to solve the internal problem, in order to move on. This main evolution defines the structural backbone of the story, much more than the dramatic action, which is usually designed as a way to get the protagonist through the conflict that is going to force them to change. This evolution has to be mapped and developed properly, as in *Silver Linings Playbook*. You'll find a detailed case study illustrating this process in the Developing a Character-Led Story chapter of *Screenwriting Unchained*.

The difference between *change* and *growth* lies in the direction and intensity of the evolution. A change means that a character is going in the wrong direction and needs to correct this. This is Melvin Uddal in *As Good As It Gets* or Sandra in *Two Days, One Night*. A growth means that a character is going in the right direction and there is nothing essentially wrong with them. They just have to get stronger, to grow. This is Billy in *Billy Elliot* or Ripley in *Alien*.

Let's take the example of two characters grieving a loss to illustrate the difference between a need to change and a need to grow. Both show an evolution, both show a "character arc", but the intensity of the change and its place in the story aren't the same.

In *Gravity* – a plot-led story – Ryan Stone has recently lost her daughter. She's in great emotional pain but she can still function. She's still able to do her job, even if that might be a way to avoid dealing with her grief. Her need to move on isn't presented as the main problem in the story. It's a character-led subplot (a problem less important than the problem in the main plot, yet connected to it) that adds depth to her character. She has a more immediate problem to deal with, which is how to survive in space when everything goes wrong and find a way back to Earth. Survival is a primal, universal need, that we understand comes before anything else and we want her to fight for it. She has to **grow** in order to reach the goal though. If she doesn't move on from her grief, she is at risk of giving up and letting herself die so that she can meet her daughter in the afterlife. A strong theme links these two forces (survival instinct, temptation to die) and delivers the central dilemma of the film. This is what makes Ryan Stone a three-dimensional character.

In *Cake* – a character-led story – Claire has also recently lost her son in a car accident. However, unlike Ryan Stone, she isn't able to function properly. Besides her chronic physical pain, she's depressed, apathetic and considering suicide. Her internal problem – the way she deals with her grief – is the main problem in the story. The main source of conflict is herself: She is her own antagonist. The fact that her life is not threatened by external characters or forces helps the audience to identify this internal, psychological problem as the main one. If she was physically struggling for survival, we would perceive this survival as the main problem because it sits lower in Maslow's pyramid of needs than self-actualisation or acceptance of facts (see Is Maslow Running the Show? in *Screenwriting Unchained*). This would make it more difficult for the audience to understand what's primarily at stake in the story. Here, as in *Two Days, One Night*, suicidal thoughts do raise the stakes, but we never wonder if the main problem is internal or external. Claire is clearly going in the wrong direction: While it's perfectly normal to grieve the death of your child, the audience hopes there is a better solution to overcome this ordeal than taking your own life. We understand her pain, especially once we have the relevant information, so we're not judging her. We are simply willing her to correct this, which is why she needs to **change**, not simply to grow.

Some characters don't need to grow and even less to change, either because they are fine as they are, or because we don't want them to change. We call these **steadfast** characters. These are the protagonists of franchises like *James Bond*, *Mission Impossible* and *Indiana Jones*. They might seem a bit two-dimensional these days, which is why franchises like *The Bourne Trilogy* were embraced: these newer films added a character journey – therefore more depth – to the protagonist. But this is also true of the main characters in a sitcom. Although most of the characters in *Friends*, *Mrs Brown* or *The Big Bang Theory* are deeply flawed, we don't want them to change because it's their flaws that make us laugh week after week.

So while you don't have to get your protagonist to change in every story, identifying the story-type of your project will help you decide whether your protagonist needs to grow, change or can remain steadfast. It will also help you to realise that other characters, even the antagonist, can change more than the protagonist. This is liberating!

Solutions

To sum it up, if you get the note that your characters are flat or two-dimensional:

✓ **Start with the protagonist** (the character who experiences the most conflict in the story, not necessarily the character who changes most), then address the other characters.

✓ **Identify the story-type of your project.** Where is the main problem located in your story? If this problem lies outside of the protagonist (in antagonistic characters or nature), you're dealing with a **plot-led story**. If the main problem sits within the protagonist, you're dealing with a **character-led story**. If the main problem lies in society and if a unique theme connects different strands with no obvious main plot, you're dealing with a **theme-led story**, a multi-stranded narrative.

If you can't identify a main problem in the story, you might be dealing with a **hybrid** or an **exception**. You will then need to ask yourself: is it a working one?

Remember, plot-led doesn't mean "with a strong plot", character-led doesn't mean "with strong characters" and theme-led doesn't mean "with a strong theme". A good story has a strong theme, a strong plot and strong characters.

If you're struggling to identify the story-type of your project and if you haven't read *Screenwriting Unchained*, you might want to download the free sampler (first fifty pages of the book). It will explain the core of the method and provide more examples. You'll find a link at the end of this book, in <u>If You Want to Find Out More...</u>

✓ **Identifying the story-type of your project should help you to define the kind of evolution you want for your protagonist, if any.** If you're dealing with a character-led story, your protagonist usually needs to **change** (the character is going in the wrong direction, they need to correct their course, often by giving up on their conscious *want* in order to reach their unconscious *need*). If you're dealing with a plot-led story, your protagonist might only need to **grow**: there is nothing wrong with the protagonist's goal or even the protagonist themselves, but they need to evolve either as a condition to reach the goal, or as a consequence of the conflict experienced during the story.

Or they might be **steadfast** characters, characters that don't need to change because we like them just the way they are.

✓   **The protagonist isn't the only character who can have an evolution.** The antagonist (main external source of conflict in a plot-led story), the catalyst (character pushing the protagonist to change in a character-led story) and other less important characters can also change or grow in your story. This might help give them more depth.

✓   **An evolution can be the evolution of a relationship between two main characters,** as in a love story or a buddy movie, or the evolution of the relationship between the protagonist and the antagonist. Such an evolution can add depth to the characters if it's well handled. Remember that characters don't need a dark trauma in their backstory to see their relationship evolve. It's about who they are rather than what happened in their past. This translates to less exposition of past events and more conflict in the present time. More on this in 18 There Is No Clear Protagonist.

✓   **To make characters three-dimensional,** check that you have clarified their goal and motivation (or lack of, as a character who doesn't want anything or who is only reactive can also be a strong character). Then define a primary character trait (this will create an archetype) as well as a few secondary character traits (this will prevent the archetype from becoming a stereotype, a cliché). If possible, find character traits that cause an internal source of conflict for the character in relation to their conscious goal or unconscious need. Think about a possible evolution for important characters, so that they are dynamic rather than static: define who they are at the beginning of the story, who they are at the end and the emotional / psychological steps that make this evolution possible and believable, ideally due to the conflict they experience. More on this in 13 The Characters Are Stereotypes or Clichés and 12 The Characters Are Too Similar.

Connected Problems in This Book

•   01 We Don't Care About the Protagonist

- 28 The Protagonist Is Not Strong Enough
- 14 The Characters' Backstories Are Irrelevant / Pointless
- 13 The Characters Are Stereotypes or Clichés
- 20 The Conflict Is Artificial or Inconsequential
- 26 The Villains or Antagonists Are Weak or Unconvincing

Sections in Screenwriting Unchained

- 1.3 Is Maslow Running the Show?
- 'Characterisation', 'Protagonist vs Antagonist', 'Protagonist vs Main Character', 'Hero vs Protagonist', 'Villain vs Antagonist' in 2.3 Craft the Draft
- 3.0 Developing a Character-Led Story

Sections in 12 Ways to a Stronger Screenplay

- Character (Change, Growth or Steadfast?)
- Antagonist or Catalyst: Who Is Testing Your Protagonist?

06 The Character Logic Is Fuzzy

This note usually means that there isn't enough causality (cause and effect) in the story. Characters' decisions are driven by what the writer needs them to do in order to serve the plot rather than acting consistently according to who they are, what they want / need or what has happened before. This could be either because the characters aren't designed properly, so anything can happen as they are no more than puppets controlled by the writer, or they are well-designed but are not always acting according to their design.

This doesn't mean that characters can't behave in a surprising way in a script, or occasionally act out of character. But if this happens, it has to make sense in the story world.

Designing characters can be compared to winding a mechanical clock or toy. You do all the design according to what you need to happen in the story, but once the story starts, it should feel like everything comes from the characters, that they react to what happens according to who they are, at that time, in the story. If you get the characters to act in a way that isn't in line with their design and previous actions, the audience will sense this external interference and the illusion will be broken.

Of course character design isn't easy, and it's closely linked to the writer's life experience and their ability to create characters who behave like human beings. Still, making sure we understand who the characters are and why they do what they do contributes to this heavily.

One thing that can help to strengthen character logic is to force yourself to look at the story from the point of view of each character, instead of looking at it from the writer's point of view, or from the protagonist's point of view. Stepping outside an objective view, or the dominant subjective view of the protagonist, can really help to ensure that the story is coherent from the point of view of all the characters involved, that they are making decisions and taking actions according to who they are and what has happened before.

This is especially true for antagonists, who rarely see themselves as antagonists (villains), but rather as the protagonists of their own story. It should also be useful if you're a male writer writing female characters, or a female writer writing male characters.

One exercise that can help to nail this is writing **character pages**: telling the story – or the backstory – over a few pages, from the point of view of each main character (protagonist, antagonist, love interest, catalyst, co-protagonist, mentor, etc). It's a great way to clarify goals / motivations and identify plot / character "holes". It's usually an enjoyable exercise that makes the character logic more consistent and hopefully will help prevent this note.

You might also tackle this problem differently depending on your project's story-type, especially if the fuzzy logic reproach is aimed at your protagonist.

If you're developing a plot-led story (where the main problem in the story lies outside the protagonist), you want to map the evolution of your protagonist and make sure that if there is a character-led subplot (often a way in which the character needs to grow), it's connected to the main plot. If the protagonist needs to grow in order to resolve the main problem, this evolution usually takes place before the climax. Other times, the growth happens as a result of the conflict experienced by the protagonist, and we see after the climax that the protagonist has evolved.

The key here is to find causality between the main plot (defined by the main conscious goal which is connected to resolving the main problem) and the character-led subplot (the character's need to grow). The conflict experienced by the character in the story should lead to the growth, and this evolution should be connected to the resolution. You can find a good example of this in *Gravity*, where Ryan Stone's goal is to survive, while her need to grow is related to the recent death of her daughter. She has to overcome her grief in order to survive, so the character's growth is closely linked to her ability to reach her goal.

If you're developing a character-led story (where the main problem in the story lies within the protagonist), the evolution of the character is usually more drastic and their need to change defines what's really at stake in the story. So you might want to look at this evolution and map it in a character breakdown: who the character is at the beginning of the story, who they are at the end, and how that change is made believable, possible and satisfying. Usually, this means having four to six main psychological or emotional steps that the character goes through as they undergo their evolution. As you map their change, you might realise that a step is missing, or that two steps are in the wrong order. Such a problem could lead to this note and a character breakdown should help you to resolve this.

This note can also stem from an unjustified negative ending. If your character fails to change, or doesn't change until it's too late, is this because they have made mistakes, they have made the wrong decisions? Can they learn, or if they die, can we learn from their failure? Is there a value in their failure for the audience? Or is it just an arbitrary ending, because the writer doesn't want a happy one?

Solutions

To sum it up, in order to address this note:

✓ **Identify the story-type of your project** (plot-led, character-led, theme-led or hybrid/exception).

✓ **If you're dealing with a plot-led story**, try to map the evolution of your protagonist. It's usually a character-led subplot that deals with a problem less important than the main problem in the story, but connected to it. This evolution is more often a growth (the character is going in the right direction, but they need to get stronger in order to reach their goal) than a change (the character is going in the wrong direction, they need to give up their conscious goal to fulfil their unconscious need).

✓ **If you're dealing with a character-led story**, the evolution of your protagonist is the backbone of your story, and defines what's really at stake. Your character unconsciously needs to change, which means they often have to let go of their conscious goal. Check that no emotional / psychological steps are missing or in the wrong order, so that the evolution is believable and satisfying. Use a character breakdown to map their evolution.

✓ **If you're developing a theme-led story (a multi-stranded narrative where the main problem usually lies in society),** you first need to identify if each strand is plot-led or character-led, and then apply the above accordingly.

✓ **Write character pages** to look at the story (and backstory) from the point of view of all the main characters, including the antagonist, so that you don't look at it solely from the writer's or the protagonist's point of view.

Connected Problems in This Book

- 25 The Narrative Is Episodic or Repetitive
- 01 We Don't Care About the Protagonist
- 38 The Plot Is Contrived
- 25 The Narrative Is Episodic or Repetitive
- 12 The Characters Are Too Similar
- 26 The Villains or Antagonists Are Weak or Unconvincing

Sections in Screenwriting Unchained

- 'Characterisation' in 2.3 Craft the Draft
- 3.0 Developing a Character-Led Story
- 4.0 Developing a Theme-Led story
- 'Character Outline', 'Character Pages', 'Evolution Map / Character Breakdown', 'Relationships Map' and 'Strands Map' in 6.2 Story Design Tools

Sections in 12 Ways to a Stronger Screenplay

- Managing Conflict (Who Wants What and Why?)
- Character (Change, Growth or Steadfast?)
- Antagonist or Catalyst (Who is Testing your Protagonist)?

07 The Story Sags in the Middle

A story sags in the middle when it runs out of steam halfway through the script.

Let's try first to understand where this problem comes from. Very often, this is a by-product of the 30–60–30 logistical approach to story structure. See the introduction of *Screenwriting Unchained* for more details on the difference between logistical and dramatic acts. You'll find a link to download a free sampler at the end of this book in If You Want to Find Out More... I also develop this in <u>19</u> <u>The Script Feels Formulaic</u>.

Because this logistical three-act paradigm is about story format rather than story structure, the narrative is cut into *logistical* acts (defined according to an arbitrary number of pages or minutes) rather than *dramatic* acts (defined according to an organic dramatic action or evolution). As a result, it's often unclear what's at stake in the story, so it becomes more difficult to sustain the main dramatic action as we reach the middle of the story.

Also, according to this logistical approach, every screenplay is supposed to have a midpoint around page sixty, and because that midpoint is often defined as a place to rest in the story, it frequently feels like we're slowing down for no reason. This is especially the case if the story was not so hectic before that we actually needed to rest. When we reach the midpoint of *John Wick*, we could do with a bit of a rest, but in less intense stories we don't necessarily need one.

So the best way to deal with a sagging midpoint is first to forget about the midpoint. We only need to rest when we're tired, and there are few stories where such a rest is actually needed. Although every single story has a middle, this midpoint is of no structural significance. Something interesting happens every few minutes in a good story, so if you look for a midpoint, you'll find one, but it doesn't mean you have to design one. A midpoint is a logistical tool, defined by the number of pages / minutes in your story. From a structural point of view, it's pretty much meaningless.

You could consider an optional mid-act climax instead, where the goal of the protagonist evolves in the second half of the story if that suits the structure of your project. For example, the protagonist spends the first half of the film seducing a woman, and once he's reached that goal, he spends the second half of the film trying to protect his family (*Life is Beautiful*). Or a group of gangsters spend the first half of the film preparing for a heist, and the second half dealing with the consequences, such as escaping the police or settling accounts (*Heat*). As long as the second goal is logically connected to the first one, as long as the second half of the story is a logical consequence of the first half, this can help structure a story that can't accommodate a single goal over the whole narrative. It might prevent the story from losing steam in the middle.

But overall, the best way to address this note is to forget entirely about *logistical* acts and rather focus on the *dramatic* structure of your story, which has nothing to do with minutes or page numbers, and everything to do with the presence (or not) of a main dramatic action and / or evolution, as this defines three dramatic acts: before, during and after the main dramatic action or evolution. Start by identifying the story-type of your project, then make full use of the fractal aspect of story structure: the fact that you can use the same three-act structure to design the whole story and its parts (acts, sequences, scenes, subplots or strands).

I don't have the space to develop this here, so if you're not familiar with the Story-Type Method and if you find reading the above slightly panic-inducing, you might want to get the free sampler of *Screenwriting Unchained*, which contains detailed info-graphs and a full introduction to the concepts summarised below. You'll find a download link in If You Want to Find Out More...

In a **plot-led story**, where the main problem sits outside of the protagonist, try to divide your story into *dramatic* units: define dramatic sequences – scenes linked together because they explore the same dramatic action – to cut your acts into self-contained mini-movies connected to each other and building on each other.

This is usually achieved using subgoals, ways for the protagonist to reach the main conscious goal.

Using dramatic units rather than logistical ones means you're much less likely to run out of steam in the middle of your story, because each dramatic sequence will propel the next one, the way each scene propels the next one. There is no set number of dramatic sequences, nor a set length for each one. You usually have four to six dramatic sequences in a dramatic Act 2, and they can be of any length that fits your story, from five to thirty minutes or more. It really doesn't matter as long as they are well-designed from a dramatic point of view and we clearly know *who wants what and why* in the sequence – and what's at stake if they fail.

Knowing what's at stake over the whole film and what's at stake in each dramatic sequence means that you can develop one strong dramatic action after the other, raising the stakes as the story unfolds, making sure that it gets harder and harder for the protagonist to obtain what they want / need and helping the audience to remain emotionally involved in the story.

In a **character-led story**, where the main problem sits within the protagonist, you'll also design dramatic sequences, but instead of sequencing a main dramatic *action*, you'll be sequencing a main dramatic *evolution*. This means that each sequence, rather than simply being a way to reach the main goal, will be designed to lead the protagonist to experience a conflict that causes the character to change, one emotional / psychological step at a time. This is because what's primarily at stake isn't what the character consciously wants, but what the character unconsciously needs. Being aware of this will help you to make sure that the evolution of the character doesn't run out of steam midway. Do you have enough steps in this evolution? Are some steps missing or in the wrong order? Getting the main evolution wrong in a character-led story can contribute to a slowing down of the narrative if we feel that nothing can be done about the internal problem of the protagonist, or if we can guess the outcome too early. This often happens in the middle of the story, potentially leading to sagging.

In a **theme-led story**, a multi-stranded narrative where the main problem tends to lie in society, you can design each strand as plot-led or character-led, and apply the principles explained above at strand level. Here, what you want to avoid is losing sight of the main theme that connects each strand, because that's the backbone of your story. If we don't see how each strand is connected to the same theme, the story will feel episodic. This can often happen in the middle of a theme-led story, because keeping the momentum in a multi-stranded narrative is a bit like keeping plates spinning on sticks: if you don't focus really hard on keeping each plate rotating fast enough on its stick, moving swiftly between each stick to keep each plate spinning, one or more will fall to the floor.

Irrespective of the story-type of your project, don't forget to look at the way you **manage information**: a few surprises, a strong dramatic irony (giving the audience information that some of the characters don't have, which can generate suspense or comedy) can help you to give your story a rocket booster when it needs it most and avoid the dreaded sagging middle syndrome. You can also shape a dramatic sequence around an ironic question (When and how will the victim of the dramatic irony find out what the audience already knows?) rather than a dramatic question (Will the protagonist of the sequence reach their subgoal?)

In a **hybrid or exception**, you might even be using a dramatic irony to shape the whole story. For example, in *The Hand That Rocks the Cradle*, we know the babysitter wants to get revenge for the death of her husband and unborn baby, the co-protagonists – the parents – don't. In *The Lives of Others*, we know the couple is being spied on by a Stasi officer; they don't. Hence any sagging middle in such a story might be related to the way you manage information rather than to the way you manage conflict.

Solutions

Expanding on this, in order to avoid the dreaded sagging middle syndrome:

✓ **Forget about any logistical approach to story** based on page numbers or minutes, with a set number of acts or sequences of fixed length, with or without associated beats or steps. Any formula based on mandatory events happening at predetermined page numbers or minutes is about story format, not story structure. More on this in <u>19 The Script Feels Formulaic.</u>

✓ Instead, **use the fractal aspect of story structure to design dramatic units** (acts, sequences, scenes, subplots or strands) in order to divide dramatic Act 2 into more manageable units that build on each other.

✓ **Identify your story-type** to find out whether you need to sequence the main dramatic action of your plot-led story, sequence the main dramatic evolution of your character-led story or sequence the strands of your theme-led story.

✓ **Look at managing information** (Who knows what when?) as well as managing conflict (Who wants / needs what and why?). A strong surprise, an intense dramatic irony, a cliffhanger (unresolved conflict) can help you prevent a sagging middle if you use them as a rocket booster for your story. In some stories, the way you manage information (forgetting to exploit a dramatic irony, resolving it too early, making a mystery last too long) could cause a sagging middle if you're not careful.

✓ **Clarify and if possible raise the stakes as the story unfolds**. To clarify the stakes in your story, answer the question: What happens if your protagonist fails to reach their conscious goal, or to find a way to change? Make sure this answer defines something we don't want to see happen to your characters, and that it becomes more and more unbearable both for the protagonist and the audience as the story progresses.

To raise the stakes, find stronger obstacles, give your antagonist a devious idea, raise the internal doubts of your protagonist or get them to make a huge *mistake* – anything that's going to increase our fear that they might fail (without taking away our hope that they might succeed). Check that the audience has all the information necessary to understand what's at stake, at all times, and that it's not just in your head.

If you don't clarify and ideally raise the stakes, the story is far more likely to sag in the middle.

✓ **Consider using a mid-act climax** if your story can't accommodate a single main dramatic action or evolution: 1) Design the first half of your story around a first dramatic goal. 2) Provide an answer to this first dramatic question during a first climax around the middle of the script. 3) In the second half of the script, explore a second dramatic question, logically connected to the first one, with another climax answering this second dramatic question towards the end.

This can prevent the story from running out of steam in the middle, for example if you don't have enough material to make a whole story out of the first dramatic action, or if you want to explore more than one problem. A classic use of this structural tool can be found in many heist stories.

Just make sure if you do use a mid-act climax that the second half is a logical consequence of the first, that the two halves are connected. Otherwise it will feel like you're telling two stories, and you might increase the sagging feeling instead of getting rid of it. If the story-type changes after a mid-act climax, you end up with a hybrid. This is what happens in *Edge of Tomorrow*: The first half is character-led (the main problem is the protagonist's cowardice), the second half is plot-led (the main problem is saving the world).

✓ **Avoid repetitions.** If your story feels episodic (a succession of unconnected events) or keeps repeating itself, if might also lead the audience to feel it's sagging. If you can take some parts of the story out or swap them around without changing anything, your story probably lacks causality (cause and effect), which is very likely to contribute to the sagging-in-the-middle feeling. More on this in 25 The Narrative Is Episodic or Repetitive.

✓ **Consider using a time-lock to raise the tension and renew the interest of the audience in the dramatic question** (Will the protagonist reach the goal or not?). A time-lock gives a limited amount of time for the protagonist to reach the goal. It's frequently used in action films (the most classic example being a ticking bomb) but it can also work in psychological dramas (for example having only *Two Days, One Night* to get your job back). You can also introduce a time-lock later in the story: The protagonist is already trying to achieve something extremely difficult when we suddenly find out that they only have a short amount of time to reach their goal. This should boost the story as it raises the stakes and provides urgency.

✓   **Don't get lost in a subplot.** If you spend too much time in a subplot (a part of the story that explores a problem less important than the main problem but connected to it), especially if it moves more slowly than the main plot, or if the protagonist of the subplot is less interesting than the protagonist of the main plot, this could also contribute to a sagging-in-the-middle feeling. It can get even worse if you get lost in more than one subplot, unless you're in a well-designed theme-led story (multi-stranded narrative). More on this in 29 The Plot Is Slowed Down By Unconnected Storylines.

Connected Problems in This Book
* 19 The Script Feels Formulaic
* 04 The Story Is Linear, Feels Predictable
* 25 The Narrative Is Episodic or Repetitive
* 16 The Scenes Are Aimless, There Is No Dramatic Conflict
* 29 The Plot Is Slowed Down By Unconnected Storylines

Sections in Screenwriting Unchained
* 1.1 What's Wrong With the Three-Act Structure?
* 'Managing Conflict' and 'Managing Information' in 2.1 Behind the Scenes
* 2.2 Sequence the Action
* 'Midpoint vs. Mid-Act Climax' and 'Time-Locks' in 2.3 Craft the Draft
* 3.2 Sequence the Evolution
* 4.2 Sequence the Strands

Sections in 12 Ways to a Stronger Screenplay
* Fractal Aspect of Story Structure
* Managing Conflict (Who Wants / Needs What and Why?)
* Managing Information (Who Knows What When?)

- Character (Change, Growth or Steadfast)
- Antagonist or Catalyst: Who Is Testing Your Protagonist?
- Time-Lock

08 The Story Is Confusing

Confusion in a story can come from a few different sources, so let's first identify the most common ones.

1) The writing style in the screenplay is confusing. The reader struggles to understand what happens because the descriptions are too long or convoluted, the character names are too similar and we keep mixing them up, etc. This is a common source of confusion, but it's also the easiest to fix, because it's about making the script easier to read as a document. Some of this confusion might disappear when the screenplay is produced, but to get there, readers have to enjoy the screenplay... So it usually has to be addressed anyway.

2) The story itself is confusing. We don't know what the story is about (the theme is unclear), who it's about (the main character isn't clear), whose story it is (the protagonist isn't clear), or we're kept in the dark about important elements in the story so we're unable to understand some of the events or the characters actions and decisions. The writer might incorrectly assume that the audience understands something, or they've forgotten to inform the audience about something. This kind of confusion will likely remain when (or if) the screenplay is produced. It's about clarity in the story design, whether the story is complex or not. It's less easy to fix, but this book is about problem-solving, so there is hope!

3) The writer wants the story to be confusing. Usually the two potential sources of confusion above aren't deliberate. However, some writers are actively looking for confusion, often using an excessive amount of mystery in order to make the story more difficult to understand. Or they might hope that an unusual structure will raise interest or make the story more challenging. This last source of confusion is harder to combat because it's part of artistic intent. Still, we'll try.

Solutions

Let's tackle these three potential sources of confusion one by one.

First, address the issue of legibility. Reading a screenplay is a more difficult process than watching a film, so you really want to make the reading process as smooth and easy as possible for the reader.

Here are a few tips towards achieving this:

✓ **Don't introduce too many characters at the same time.** Also, try to give a couple of visual elements in the first description of each character to help the reader remember who is who.

✓ **Make sure that characters don't have similar names,** as we might confuse them, especially at the beginning of the story.

✓ If you're looking for development or production partners in other countries, **verify that your character names are not too difficult to read or memorise for a reader who doesn't speak your language / share your culture.** If at all possible, use easier-to-read nicknames.

✓ **Watch out for places, signs, references to historical events that might have an obvious meaning in your culture but are completely unknown to a foreign reader / audience.** When we see the arm of the Statue of Liberty at the end of *Planet of the Apes*, we probably don't need any help to understand that this used to be New York, even for those who don't live in the U.S. or speak English. You might be trying to give such a visual clue in your story, without realising it's only meaningful to a tiny part of your intended audience. If these elements are important in order to understand the story, find a way to dramatise this meaning through action or dialogue so that it reaches the audience, not only the reader, unless you're confident it will become visually clear once on screen.

✓ **Avoid long sentences except when you want to slow down the pace of the story.** The faster the action, the shorter the sentences. Read just about any script by James Cameron, Jane Goldman, Tony Gilroy or Kathryn Bigelow to get a sense of this.

✓   **Make sure that everything is clear in your descriptions so readers don't have to stop and re-read.** Anything that gets in the way of reading the script gets in the way of experiencing the story.

✓   **Try to be visual in your descriptions**, but don't spend paragraphs describing locations, costumes or objects in detail unless these elements are significant to the story.

Then, address sources of confusion in the story design itself. This is a wide subject and almost every section in this book explores some aspect of it. However, here are two of the most important areas to focus on:

✓   **Focus on the way you manage conflict (Who wants / needs what and why?) in your story.** Whose story is it? Do you have a clear protagonist, with a clear main dramatic action or evolution, or is your story a multi-stranded narrative, with each strand connected to the same theme? Identifying the story-type of your project will help you tremendously and is the first step toward reaching clarity in your story design. This is the essence of the Story-Type Method, so if you need help with this, please take a look at the free resources linked in If You Want to Find Out More... at the end of this book.

✓   **Look at the way you manage information (Who knows what when?) in your story.** Sometimes, a writer can take a piece of information for granted, or can forget to convey it to the audience, which becomes a source of confusion. Some writers also resist sharing information with the audience. They might rely almost exclusively on mystery (the writer knows something that the audience doesn't) instead of using other tools as well, such as dramatic irony (the audience knows something that at least one character doesn't), surprise or suspense. This can lead to confusion after a while, because we don't know enough about what happens in the story, or why a protagonist makes certain decisions. Mystery might draw us in intellectually, but it makes it harder for the audience to get emotionally involved, which increases the risk of confusion and boredom. A good story finds the right balance between intellectual and emotional gratification. It's not the same for all stories, but weighing too much on the intellectual side often prevents us from delivering on the emotional side.

Finally, address intentional confusion:

✓ **Don't be afraid of clarity.** Some writers deliberately try to create confusion because they don't want their story to be too easy to understand. This might be because they believe a story has to be cryptic or at the very least complex to wow critics or arthouse festivals. Yet simplicity isn't the same as being simplistic. Simplicity and clarity are the most difficult things to achieve. True masters of any art form pursue them for this very reason.

✓ **Complexity isn't the same as confusion.** Writing a confusing screenplay is extremely easy. Usually, it won't get made or will reach a limited audience. What's difficult is to design a complex story which is nevertheless clear, and to create complex characters whose evolution is meaningful. This can be a way to reach a crossover audience. The fact that a movie can be understood by everyone doesn't make it any less valuable from an artistic point of view. The fact that only a handful of people can decipher it doesn't give it more artistic value either.

✓ **Whether you're after simplicity or complexity, aim for clarity and try to avoid confusion**. A story can be intellectually challenging as long as it's also emotionally rewarding. To achieve both, you need clarity, for the writer *and* the audience. Seek complexity in the design. For example, create a working exception or a hybrid if you find more common story-types too straightforward. Deliver a unique story that works at an emotional level, even if its design is complex and unconventional, instead of making it a cold, confusing intellectual puzzle.

Connected Problems in This Book

- 18 There Is No Clear Protagonist
- 06 The Character Logic Is Fuzzy
- 34 Too Many Questions Are Left Unanswered
- 35 The Script Is Unnecessarily Complex

Sections in Screenwriting Unchained

- To explore how complex stories can nevertheless achieve clarity, see the case studies of *Gravity*, *Silver Linings Playbook*, *The Intouchables*, *Crash*, *Cloud Atlas* and all the hybrids and exceptions: *Edge of Tomorrow*, *The Lives of Others*, *Birdman*, *The Secret in Their Eyes*, *L.A. Confidential*.

Sections in 12 Ways to a Stronger Screenplay

- Story-Type and Genre
- M-Factor (What's at Stake?)
- Theme
- Set-Up / Story World
- Satisfying Ending

09 The Screenplay Is Too Dry or Not Visual Enough

Writing only what we're going to see or hear on screen doesn't mean we have to do so in a way that's robotic or dull. We can make action sequences thrilling, comedy scenes funny and dramatic moments intense using the appropriate writing style.

What you don't want to do is give the reader information that will never reach the audience (for example, describe the character's internal thoughts or emotions). However, there's nothing wrong with writing a brief description of a character the first time they appear, using a few words to encapsulate the essence of the character if that's going to be obvious in the behaviour of the character and in the acting in the following scenes.

You can't write backstory elements in descriptions – whether we learn about them later or not – but you can slightly cheat and write something that's going to be obvious in the next scene, if it helps the reader to picture the character. It's always a good idea to show as much visually as possible, as this is what translates to the screen.

For example, don't write:

```
John McClane, 37, a wisecracking New
York cop who is afraid of flying and
is recently separated from his wife.
```
But it's fine to write:

```
On John McClane: good-looking, mid-
thirties, athletic and tired from
his trip. He sits by the window. His
relief on landing is subtle, but we
NOTICE.
```
This is the description of the protagonist of *Die Hard* the first time we see him. We don't need more than that at this stage. Just a way to picture the character when we meet him as we read the script.

Moments later, we'll find out that he's a cop through a funny interaction with a passenger. A bit later on, we'll learn that he is recently separated from his wife, again through action and dialogue, not in a literary description.

You can even go a bit further if what's in the description is going to be obvious in the acting and directing. For example, here's the description of Richard, the father in *Little Miss Sunshine*, the first time we meet him:

```
Richard (45), stands at the front of
a community college classroom —
cinderblock walls, industrial
carpeting. He wears khaki shorts, a
golf shirt, sneakers. He moves with
the stocky, stiff-legged gait of a
former athlete. His peppy, upbeat
demeanour just barely masks a
seething sense of insecurity and
frustration.
```

In this example, there is a bit of backstory and a hint of the main character traits in the last sentence, but it's shown visually. The clothes he's wearing, the location contribute to tell us a lot about the character. We believe that a good actor will be able to convey Richard's frustration and sense of insecurity despite his upbeat demeanour, and that's exactly what Greg Kinnear does. And it's visual, so there is no cheating with excessive literary information.

Solutions

✓ **Find the right balance** between writing a literary script — full of information about the plot or the characters that will never reach the audience, or would only reach the audience much later in the story — and penning a super-dry script written in telegraphic style that feels as dead and impersonal as the phone book.

You want to stick mostly to what we see and hear on screen, but write it in the most entertaining, surprising, truthful way. You can and should use an *effective* style when writing a script, just not a *literary* style.

✓ **Avoid "plain" verbs to indicate physical movement or action.** Instead select the most appropriate word to suggest the exact nuance or feeling. To sit isn't the same as to slouch or to drop in a chair. To run, to rush and to dash also suggest different actions and emotions.

✓ **Use visual storytelling as much as possible.** Show rather than tell. Assign a specific meaning to an object earlier in the story so that when we see the object again in a specific situation, we understand what the character feels, like C.C. Baxter finding out that the woman he loves is his boss's mistress simply by recognising her broken mirror in *The Apartment*.

Although the above should be useful, nothing beats learning from actual screenplays – written by masters of the genre that interests you – to tell a visual story on paper effectively. If Billy Wilder and I.A.L. Diamond aren't your cup of tea, how about James Cameron if you're a sci-fi fan? His screenplays for *Terminator 2: Judgment Day* or *Aliens* are great examples of his effective writing style, where each paragraph tends to suggest a shot. Another inspiring writer, especially for action movies, is Tony Gilroy, who adapted the *Bourne Trilogy* from Robert Ludlum's novels. Jane Goldman (*Kick Ass*, *Kingsman : The Secret Services*) blends action and humour in a unique way. If you want to write exciting action scenes, you'll learn a lot from these writers. Shorter sentences as the pace of the story speeds up, very visual storytelling, yet three-dimensional characters.

The late William Goldman (*Misery*, *Butch Cassidy and the Sundance Kid*) is another great source of inspiration for his economical yet effective style. He writes strong characters and fantastic dialogue. If you like character-led stories, screenplays by David O. Russel are worth studying, especially his adaptation of *Silver Linings Playbook*. Diablo Cody (*Juno*, *Young Adult*, *Tully*) is another writer who can teach us lot about designing great characters and revealing who they are through both action and dialogue. If you prefer comedies erring on the gross out / parodic side, take a look at Katie Dippold's work (*The Heat*, *Ghostbusters 2016*).

Read their work to see how they did it. Then find your own style.

Connected Problems in This Book

- 11 The Screenplay Is Written Like a Novel
- 30 The Script Contains Too Much Exposition
- 21 There Is Too Much Dialogue
- 31 The Drama / Conflict Is Told But Not Shown

Sections in Screenwriting Unchained

- 'Visual storytelling', 'Planting and Pay-Off' and 'Flashbacks: To FB or Not to FB?' in 2.3 Craft the Draft
- *Gravity* in 2.5 Case Studies
- *Silver Linings Playbook* in 3.5 Case Studies
- *Crash* in 4.5 Case Studies
- 'Scene Breakdown' in 6.2 Story Design Tools

Sections in 12 Ways to a Stronger Screenplay

- Planting, Pay-Off and Visual Storytelling

10 The Ending Doesn't Work

This one is a bummer. The ending is what you leave the audience with. It's crucial in terms of generating both meaning and a positive word-of-mouth. The last thing we want in a story is an ending that doesn't work.

Solving this problem is often hindered by the passionate debate around happy ending vs. unhappy ending.

Some filmmakers believe that we need a happy ending to have a commercially successful movie. Others believe that without an unhappy ending, they can't create an artistic piece. Both sides can be equally wrong.

What matters in a story isn't whether the ending is happy or unhappy, but whether or not it's satisfying.

In a thriller, you can rarely kill off your protagonist because the movie is about survival against all odds. Killing the protagonist goes against the genre, unless it's a sacrifice that allows others to survive. Otherwise, it's neither meaningful, nor satisfying. Just an artificial, unsatisfying surprise.

On the other hand, in a true tragedy – a story exploring a tragic flaw in a character – a failure to learn or change or even the death of the protagonist is often needed to bring a satisfying, meaningful ending.

The problem is that tacking on a happy ending when the ending should be sad in order to be meaningful is just as wrong as forcing an unhappy ending because "it's less commercial, hence more artistic". The section about happy ending vs satisfying ending in *Screenwriting Unchained* might be helpful if you'd like to explore this further.

It could also be that the ending isn't actually the problem but a symptom. It's towards the end that the problem becomes most visible, but if we simply focus on the symptom, we'll just get different versions of an ending that still doesn't work.

An unsatisfying ending can be due to a plot problem. For example, the main dramatic question isn't raised clearly in a **plot-led story** (where the main problem lies outside of the protagonist) so it's almost impossible to find a satisfying answer during the climax.

It can also be rooted in theme – when the theme isn't defined clearly enough, or when strands aren't connected sufficiently to the same theme in a **theme-led movie** (a multi-stranded narrative where the main problem often lies in society).

An ending can also be unsatisfying because it's not emotionally moving. This is usually because it's trying to show a conceptually moving situation instead of paying off what happened before in the story. For example, we believe that the death of a character will be moving, but if we don't care about that character, if we don't know them well enough, if this death doesn't pay off a characterisation or an evolution, the ending will fall flat. This is because it relies on a conceptually moving situation (someone dying) that would have the same value in any story irrespective of what happened previously.

In any case, you first need to check whether the ending not working is a symptom or a problem, otherwise your chances of fixing this one are fairly remote.

Sometimes an unsatisfying ending comes from a writer setting up a main problem in the story that can't find a satisfying solution. It might create a great dilemma and a lot of conflict in the story, but in the end, you leave the audience with an unsolved problem, which often leads to an unsatisfying ending. For example, if the protagonist's goal is to solve world hunger or to achieve world peace, it's going to be hard to find a satisfying, believable, meaningful ending. If your protagonist is dying of a terminal disease, better not make survival the main problem in the story, or it will end depressingly or with a *deus ex machina* – an unexplained, unlikely and unexpected recovery!

In this case, a possible solution would be to define a solvable problem – at story level – so that you can deliver a satisfying ending even if the thematic problem isn't solved. For example, while a character might be dying, what's at stake in the movie – the main problem – could be defined as an emotional change for the protagonist, as in *The Fault in Our Stars*, or as something more important than the survival of the protagonist, as in *Leaving Las Vegas*.

Another solution to this issue might be to go for a **theme-led story (a multi-stranded narrative)**, so that you don't unrealistically solve the main problem in the story – how drugs are threatening western society in *Traffic*, racial tension in L.A. in *Crash* – but show how some of the characters in some of the strands find a way to deal with the problem at an individual level, even if the problem as a whole remains present in society.

That way, your story doesn't have to be depressing (as expected, the problem can't be solved) or unrealistic (unexpectedly and miraculously, the problem is artificially solved) but you can still have a balanced approach with some of the characters in some strands managing to find a solution or overcome the problem, and others being unable to do so.

In a **character-led story**, an unsatisfying ending is often tied to the evolution of the protagonist, because we might not have made the distinction between what the character *wants* consciously and what they *need* unconsciously. The protagonist of a character-led story often has to give up their conscious goal in order to reach their unconscious need. In *Silver Linings Playbook*, Pat gives up trying to get back together with Nicky (his conscious *want* over the whole story) and that allows him to get what he *needs* (to move on, get better and be with Tiffany). Sandra in *Two Days, One Night* gives up trying to get her job back (her conscious *want* over the whole story), and that allows her to get what she *needs*: her self-esteem back. In both cases, this failure on the protagonist's conscious goal provides success on their unconscious need, which is what was really at stake in the story, hence a satisfying ending.

Solutions

To sum it up, in order to get a better ending:

✓ **Forget about happy endings and unhappy endings. Focus instead on finding a *satisfying* ending.** An ending doesn't work when it's unsatisfying. The same event can cause different reactions in different stories. For example, the death of a protagonist can be rejected if unjustified, or can move us to tears if it's the only meaningful way to end the story.

✓ **Identify the story-type of your project (plot-led, character-led, theme-led, hybrid or exception).** When the ending doesn't work, it's often because the writer isn't clear about story-type and doesn't know which dramatic or thematic question they need to answer, or what was primarily at stake in the story.

✓ **Make a distinction between what the protagonist *wants* and what the protagonist *needs*.** Often, especially in character-led stories, protagonists have to give up what they want in order to obtain what they need. Being clear about which of these is primarily at stake in each story should help you to reach a satisfying ending.

✓ **Remember that a protagonist doesn't have to succeed** (to reach the goal, or to change) for the ending to be satisfying. If a protagonist can learn from their mistakes, if the audience can learn from their death or failure, we can accept a negative ending.

✓ However, **if your protagonist fails at the end of the story, remember that by then we have become the protagonist** thanks to the identification process. When you hit them on the head, the audience feels the blow. If the protagonist has made the wrong decisions, we can accept this failure and even be moved by it as long as we understand why. Otherwise, we'll feel it's unjust and we'll likely reject the ending.

✓ **Beware: The audience has an innate sense of justice.** Whether it's positive or negative, does the protagonist deserve the ending? Given the choices, the decisions, the efforts made by the protagonist, does the ending feel fair? This is not about being realistic. It's about fairness. An undeserved punishment works very well to create identification at the beginning of a story (*The Fugitive*). It's unlikely to work at the end, unless it's not perceived as a punishment but as a choice, a result of free will (*Thelma & Louise*).

✓   **Forget about realism**. Life isn't fair, and anything can happen to us at any time, even if we don't deserve it. This is terrifying. When we pay for a story, we're buying the illusion that what we do matters, that if we try hard enough, we can succeed, that we get what we (feel we) deserve. Or that if we make mistakes, we pay the price. A satisfying ending often gives the audience the *illusion* that they have some control over their lives, or that evil doesn't remain unpunished. It's not always realistic, but it's comforting and satisfying. If you don't deliver this, make sure that you deliver something else equally valuable. For example, at the end of *Se7en*, Detective Mills kills antagonist John Doe, which completes the serial killer's task: Doe's sin was envy (he envied Mills' "normal" life) and Mills' sin is wrath. This ending isn't comforting: not only does the antagonist win, but both Mills' and Somerset's lives are wrecked. It's disturbing, bleak, yet intellectually satisfying, because we realise the extent of Doe's planning. It's also emotionally satisfying, because the ending is full of suspense, tension, surprises and ultimately pity and compassion for Mills. The audience is shocked, upset, but the story puzzle is solved in such a way that we can only admire the design.

✓   **Make sure the ending pays off the whole story**. The most moving endings are planted by what happens before and they often use visual storytelling to pay off such elements. For example, at the end of *City Lights*, the flower girl realises that the man who gave her money to restore her eyesight isn't the generous millionaire she thought he was, but a penniless tramp. This pays off the whole story, and it's the visual resolution of a strong dramatic irony (we knew all along that he had no money, she didn't).

✓   **Avoid an anti-climax or a deus ex machina** (see these two connected problems in the list below).

Connected Problems in This Book

* 08 The Story Is Confusing
* 17 The Script Loses the Plot in the Third Act

- 22 The Ending Is an Anti-Climax
- 23 The Ending Is a *Deus Ex Machina*
- 34 Too Many Questions Are Left Unanswered
- 13 The Characters Are Stereotypes or Clichés

Sections in Screenwriting Unchained

- 'Climax vs Ending' and 'Happy Ending vs Satisfying Ending' in 2.3 Craft the Draft
- 'Avoiding a Deus ex Machina in *Gravity*' in 2. Developing a Plot-Led Story

Sections in 12 Ways to a Stronger Screenplay

- Crafting a Satisfying Ending: moving, entertaining and meaningful

11 The Screenplay Is Written Like a Novel

This chilling statement is issued when writers with a literary background rely too much on the written word and not enough on dramatic language, which lies in the underlying design and story structure.

A screenplay can be very pleasant, meaningful, complex, even moving, but for the wrong reasons, i.e. for literary reasons. If a screenplay keeps stating what the characters think or feel, as in a novel, it might help the reader to understand what's going on in the character's mind and get emotionally involved in the story, but it won't help the audience because what's on the page doesn't end up on the screen. The reader might weep or laugh or be amazed at such depth, sensitivity, humour and wit, but the audience might well be bored stiff.

We have to dramatise (through action and dialogue) what the audience needs to understand before they can be involved in the story. Writing a thought or an emotion in the screenplay that can only be read in a description doesn't help the audience.

Also, some novels might be perceived as being visual because they describe beautiful scenery or picturesque events, but if the emotions in the story rely primarily on the internal thoughts or feelings of the characters, it will take a lot of work to translate this to the screen.

Many adaptations hit that wall. The fact that they create strong mental images on the page doesn't necessarily mean they are good candidates for film or TV. Pages, characters and subplots may have been cut to make the story fit into a shorter format, but the real adaptation work – deciding how a story designed to be read has to be changed to work on the screen – hasn't been done. It might look like a screenplay on the surface, but underneath it's still a literary work.

Solutions

How can you prevent this note?

✓ **Make sure that your story is dramatic and not literary in essence.** Are you telling the story through dramatic actions and / or evolutions, which generate emotion because events are dramatised? Or are you delivering a diary of the internal thoughts and feelings of a character, using literary descriptions or voiceover?

✓ **Is someone, a character or a group of characters sharing the same goal, trying to do something about a problem, consciously or not?** Have you identified the dramatic engine of the story by assessing its story-type: **plot-led** if the main problem lies outside of the protagonist, **character-led** if the main problem lies within the protagonist, **theme-led** if the main problem lies in society, leading to a multi-stranded narrative? If it's a **hybrid or exception,** do you know how it's going to work at a dramatic level?

✓ **Most novels can't be adapted to the screen without designing a new dramatic story engine,** because they either don't have one or have too many. This is especially true of novels with a beautiful literary style, or novels that explore a subject that is, in essence, literary: biographies or stories that rely on a non-visual sensory element, such as Patrick Süskind's *Perfume.*

✓ **Try to describe mostly what we'll see and hear on screen.** If something written in the script will only reach the reader and not the audience, find a way to dramatise it using action and dialogue if it's important, otherwise get rid of it. Don't go too far in this direction though or you might end up with another problem: 09 The Screenplay Is Too Dry or Not Visual Enough.

✓ **Refrain from writing about the thoughts and feelings of the characters,** whether in the descriptions or in dialogue.

People rarely talk directly about their thoughts and feelings. Dialogue should help us to understand how they feel or what they think (thanks to subtext, what the characters mean but *don't* say). If they actually state their feelings, the dialogue may well be flagged as "on the nose".

Instead, try to express this through the characters' actions or reactions, and use planting and payoff to create visual storytelling: Assign a specific meaning to an object, character, song or even line of dialogue, so that you can convey meaning visually when you pay this off later in the story. Watch the broken mirror sequence in *The Apartment* to see a classic example of how it is done.

✓ **Remember, using flashbacks won't necessarily make your story more cinematic, original or exciting.** Unless you master the art of non-linear storytelling, you are more likely to raise alarm bells in experienced readers (for one successful flashback structure, there are ninety-nine failed ones) and bore the audience. Flashbacks can be a great tool as an alternative to exposition, they can even create fantastic narratives based on a non-linear structure if the writer gets it right, but they are rarely an efficient crutch if the writer hasn't mastered dramatic writing in the first place.

Connected Problems in This Book

* 09 The Screenplay Is Too Dry or Not Visual Enough
* 27 The Script Is Cold, Unemotional
* 30 The Script Contains Too Much Exposition
* 25 The Narrative Is Episodic or Repetitive
* 31 The Drama / Conflict Is Told But Not Shown
* 29 The Plot Is Slowed Down By Unconnected Storylines
* 02 We Don't Care About the Story

Sections in Screenwriting Unchained

* 1.3 Is Maslow Running the Show?
* 2.1 Behind the Scenes
* 'Flashbacks: To FB or Not to FB' in 2.3 Craft the Draft

- 6.2 Story Design Tools

Sections in 12 Ways to a Stronger Screenplay
- Story-Type and Genre
- M-Factor (What's at Stake?)
- Fractal Aspect of Story Structure
- Planting, Pay-Off and Visual Storytelling

12 The Characters Are Too Similar

This note can arise for a variety of reasons, the most common being when all the characters speak and behave like the writer: all the characters directly express through dialogue the writer's point of view or what the writer wants to say, instead of conveying this indirectly through their actions and evolutions.

Although such a monochromatic writing style might have worked occasionally in the past, for example in comedy, it's rarely effective today. Even if the writers – hence the characters – are witty or funny, it feels unrealistic, which can make it difficult for a contemporary audience to engage with any of the characters.

Another reason for this note turning up might be that we have a group of characters who all behave in the same way (not necessarily like the writer). For example, in an action movie, we have a group of co-protagonists, but they are more or less interchangeable. Or in a multi-stranded narrative, we have various strands but the characters are too similar to make the most of what this unconventional story design has to offer when used efficiently.

One of the main benefits of creating characters who are not similar is that it creates contrast, hence conflict or complementarity. For example, when we have co-protagonists, designing characters who are radically different means that they can argue about the way to reach the goal, or even undermine the other's success because of their differences. Think about the crew of the Nostromo in *Alien*, the trio of co-protagonists in *Jaws*, or the co-protagonists in *The Avengers*. All the characters share the same goal (surviving in *Alien*, killing the shark in *Jaws*, saving the world in *The Avengers*), yet they are all very different. The co-protagonists occasionally disagree, sometimes at a fundamental level, which creates suspense, surprises, opposition and, ultimately, complementarity when they find a way to work together in order to reach their goal.

This is also true in comedy, especially in ensemble pieces such as *Friends*, *Bridesmaids* or *The Hangover*. What makes us laugh is the conflict generated by the contrast between very different characters, and the way they can unite and become stronger when facing adversity.

This is the essence of any buddy movie (*The Heat*, *The Intouchables*, *Planes Trains and Automobiles*, *Midnight Run*). Two characters in complete opposition, who might end up learning from each other before becoming best friends.

Solutions

Here are a few tips to help you resolve this problem:

✓ **Define one main character trait for each character (not just the protagonist) and a few secondary traits**. The first trait will define an archetype; the additional traits will contribute to making this archetype unique. This should help you to get a clear handle on each character as they face a conflict, make a decision or talk to each other. It might also help you to write their dialogue – more than having pages of random character backstory.

✓ **Use conflict to reveal who your characters are**. We tend to behave similarly when there is no conflict. Find the conflict that will reveal, through action and dialogue, the inner essence of your characters.

✓ **Define a goal (conscious want and / or unconscious need) and motivation for each character**, not just the protagonist and antagonist. What a character wants or needs is one of the most defining characteristics in a human being, in real life as in fiction. Two characters might want the same thing for different reasons, which will make them very different.

✓ **Check that the characters are different on the page and not only in your head.** Cover the character names in the script, in the action and in the dialogue and ask a friend to read a few pages. Can they figure out who is who simply by looking at what the character does and says? If they can't, that might be part of the problem.

✓ **Don't rely on accents or dialects to correct this issue.** First, because characters in a given story often have no reason to exhibit a different accent or dialect, but also because it's very annoying to read dialogue with a "baked in" accent or dialect, which often comes across as clichéd. If there is a reason to have this, for example if characters in your story do come from different backgrounds, then indicate their accent in parenthesis below the character's name and let the actor handle it. Choose the words and the locutions to suggest the dialect, but don't write the accent literally on the page.

Second, because more than the way someone speaks, it's what they choose to say that often defines them. For example, instead of specifying "with a farmer's accent", which doesn't mean much, have the character talk about the crops, the seasons or farming machinery. Something that only someone who lives and works on a farm would know. This will be a lot more efficient than giving a character an artificial accent or dialect.

✓ **Hunt mercilessly for unnecessary exposition.** As you make your characters different, you'll have to convey these specific character traits to the audience. Don't rely on exposition to achieve that, especially if it relates to backstory. We have exposition when characters talk about what happened before the story started, or about events that took place in between scenes but weren't shown. We also have exposition when characters talk about their feelings or intentions, or what's happening in the story, when we should be able to figure it out by ourselves. Actors will turn down a script if their part is full of exposition, or they will do all they can to have it cut down. As your screenplay will only be produced if it gets a cast, and preferably a good one, do yourself a favour and go on an exposition hunt.

✓ **Use visual storytelling.** This is an efficient way to reduce the amount of exposition. Instead of having characters talk about past events, plot developments, inner emotions, find ways to show this visually. This usually involves planting and pay-off, or possibly the use of flashbacks as an alternative to exposition if there is no other way around it. The best way to convey a specific character trait to the audience is to find a conflictual situation that reveals it. If your character is jealous, generous or reckless, show it, don't tell it. This is true for each of the character traits, but also for the evolution of each character.

Connected Problems in This Book

- 13 The Characters Are Stereotypes or Clichés
- 05 The Characters Are Flat, Two-Dimensional
- 14 The Characters' Backstories Are Irrelevant / Pointless
- 30 The Script Contains Too Much Exposition
- 31 The Drama / Conflict Is Told But Not Shown
- 39 The Theme Overshadows the Story

Sections in Screenwriting Unchained

- 'Visual Storytelling' in 2.1 Behind the Scenes
- 'Characterisation' and 'Flashbacks: To FB or Not to FB?' in 2.3 Craft the Draft
- 3.0 Developing a Character-Led Story
- 4.0 Developing a Theme-Led story
- 6.2 Story Design Tools

Sections in 12 Ways to a Stronger Screenplay

- Character (Change, Growth or Steadfast?)
- Planting, Pay-Off and Visual Storytelling

13 The Characters Are Stereotypes or Clichés

This one is interesting because it touches on the difference between archetypes (characters with a classic function, such as hero, sidekick or mentor, which can be useful in some stories) and stereotypes or clichés (characters that we have seen a thousand times before, such as the prostitute with a heart of gold, the conflicted action movie protagonist with a dead or estranged spouse, the villain with a traumatic childhood, etc).

Three key points to deal with this note

1) If your characters feel stereotypical, it's most likely because you're offering "the same, but the same", not "the same, but different". Copying what's been done before, following a well-established formula, is boring. That's painting by numbers. The dead wife cliché worked in *Lethal Weapon* because it wasn't a cliché then. The "guilt over a fateful event" worked in *Cliffhanger* but it doesn't cut it today. We've seen it far too many times. At the same time, doing something that's never been done before can make producers and distributors nervous.

So we're usually looking for a reassuring degree of familiarity, but an equal degree of innovation and originality. A convention often exists because it works, but if you follow it, audiences want to see something fresh. In *John Wick*, the protagonist hasn't simply lost his wife (cliché), he's angry because the bad guys killed the dog his wife gave him as a present "from beyond the grave". Granted, it's a bit silly, but it had never been done before and it sets the right tone for the film: an action thriller full of self-deprecating humour. The cliché establishes the genre and gives the audience a shortcut to identification. Making fun of it doesn't insult our intelligence and creates instead a kind of complicity. In other words, the same, but different.

2) The main way out of this is to keep the archetype if it helps you to tell the story (i.e. it serves a story function), but find a way to make the archetype unique, so that it feels like a character we've never seen before.

A good way to achieve this is to define a clear main psychological trait for each character. This will often define an archetype. For example, Salieri in *Amadeus* is jealous; Mildred Hayes in *Three Billboards* is persistent; Indiana Jones in *Raiders* is adventurous; Nurse Annie in *Misery* is psychotic.

Then find a couple of traits that are going to make this archetype unique. For example, Salieri loves food and is talented enough to recognise Mozart's talent, but not talented enough to match it, which feeds both his admiration for Mozart and his jealousy. Mildred is also grieving, angry and she's a rebel. Indy is a professor of archaeology, is scared of snakes and features a distinctive bullwhip and hat. Annie is Paul Sheldon's number one fan, she has a pet pig called Misery and she is a baby killer.

If we handle characters like this, we can still have strong archetypes: a jealous protagonist, yet very different from Othello; a strong-willed female protagonist who never gives up; an action hero unlike all those we had seen before; a psychotic villain who inspired many clichés but wasn't one when she was created. Still, none of them is a stereotype.

3) Forget about formulas. The protagonist isn't necessarily "the character who changes most in a story". We don't always want the characters to change, even if they are flawed, because we might like them just the way they are. In a sitcom for example, the characters' flaws could be what make us laugh. In *The Big Bang Theory*, we don't want the characters to change, despite their obvious flaws. Change the characters, give them an "arc", and you lose the comedy. This is what happens at the end of *Friends*: they become grown-ups, they change, but only because it's time to end the show. So don't feel like you have to force a character arc for all the main characters in every story.

Solutions

Let's start with a less dogmatic definition. As explained in 01 We Don't Care About the Protagonist, the protagonist is the character who experiences the most conflict in a story.

This has different implications according to the story-type:

In a plot-led story, the main problem lies outside the protagonist. Sure, the protagonist can have a flaw, there might be a character-led subplot, but it doesn't have to be the cliché of the dead partner or the guilt trauma. This kind of backstory is a shortcut to give conflict to the protagonist right away, before the action even starts. This can help us identify with the character, by making them less perfect, more human. But if it's a cliché, it won't help much. Better find a possible internal obstacle, such as Chief Brody's fear of water in *Jaws*, something that will make it more difficult for this character to resolve this specific story problem, rather than a conceptual conflict (loss of a loved one) and a cliché.

Many story theoreticians insist on a character arc even when it's not needed. So freeing yourself from this in plot-led stories could be a first step to avoiding a cliché. Granted, a modern audience expects more complex characters than James Bond or Indiana Jones, but if they wanted really complex or conflicted characters, they'd be watching a character-led story, not an action thriller or an adventure film. Plot-led stories meet a larger audience because they make it look like we bear no responsibility for most of the problems we face. This simplistic way of looking at life is reassuring for many. Making them too much like character-led stories means that the story doesn't serve this comforting purpose anymore. So if you want a character-led subplot in your plot-led story, keep it under control: a growth is usually fine, a change can be a step too far and might lead to a stereotype or a cliché.

In a character-led story, however, the character who changes most *is* usually the protagonist, because what's primarily at stake is whether the protagonist will change or not, whether they will control their inner flaw or will resolve their internal problem. And because we resist change, we need conflict to force the character to evolve. This is a complex process, so I won't detail it here, but it's fundamentally different from plot-led stories. If you've not read

Screenwriting Unchained, see <u>If You Want to Find Out More...</u> at the end of this book to download the free sampler and learn more about these differences. With character-led stories, you're at risk of ending up with a different set of clichés.

The main one is "the flawed character who deserves to make it but won't because a happy ending is supposed to be too commercial". We see a character with an inner problem, who struggles and gradually changes, and even makes the right decisions during the story, but the writer gives an artificial, unhappy ending to the story (and a depressing outcome for the character).

The problem is that when we identify with a protagonist over the whole film, we become the character. If we make the wrong decisions, we can accept being punished if it helps us learn from our mistakes. But the audience will reject an undeserved punishment for the protagonist, because we become a victim of that injustice too. Sure, undeserved punishment can happen in real life, but why pay for something we can have for free?

The power of drama isn't to show life as it is. That's what documentaries do. It's either to show life as we would like it to be ("If you try hard enough, you will succeed", "Good triumphs over evil", "Love conquers all", etc) or to help us understand life, the human psyche, why we make mistakes and how to avoid repeating them.

Both types of stories help us to deal with the harshness of life. One in an escapist way, the other in a deeper, more sophisticated way. But there is a healing power in both approaches.

So if you're dealing with a character-led story, make sure you're providing a satisfying ending if you want to avoid disappointing the audience. It can be happy or unhappy, but it has to be satisfying, and to be satisfying we have to be able to learn something from it. More on this in <u>10 The Ending Doesn't Work</u>. If you're struggling with this, it might be because your screenplay could be better developed as a theme-led story.

A theme-led story is a multi-stranded narrative where the main problem usually lies in society. Often, this problem can't be resolved. There isn't one protagonist over the whole story, as there isn't one character – or group of characters – experiencing more conflict than the others. There is no main plot as there is no main dramatic action or evolution. There can't be subplots when there is no main plot, so we call each storyline a strand.

However, you can certainly have a protagonist for each strand, and handle each strand as plot-led (the main problem in the strand lies outside the protagonist) or character-led (the main problem in the strand lies within the protagonist).

We tend to end up with clichés in theme-led stories when the characters feel artificial because they only exist to convey the theme, or because they show an extreme attitude or illustrate an extreme point of view in relation to the theme.

For example, in a multi-stranded narrative about drugs, you might only involve cops and drug dealers. It might be more exciting to do what Steven Soderbergh does in *Traffic*, and show not only drug dealers and drug enforcement officers, but drug users, a drug czar who happens to be the father of a young addict, the wife of a drug dealer who had no idea her husband was trafficking, etc. It offers a wider palette of situations and viewpoints, all connected to the same theme. Christopher Nolan does something similar in *Dunkirk*, finding characters – heroes but also cowards and deserters – that go against expectations in a war movie.

In other words, a theme-led story allows you to explore a world in shades of grey. It's an option worth exploring if you can't find a satisfying ending when you handle your story as plot-led or character-led. With a theme-led story, the filmmaker's vision or point of view is expressed through a multitude of endings, some positive, some negative. If the problem you're exploring lies in society, most often it can't be solved realistically in a two-hour fiction.

Connected Problems in This Book

- 12 The Characters Are Too Similar
- 05 The Characters Are Flat, Two-Dimensional
- 06 The Character Logic Is Fuzzy
- 01 We Don't Care About the Protagonist
- 26 The Villains or Antagonists Are Weak or Unconvincing
- 10 The Ending Doesn't Work
- 15 The Dialogue Is Cheesy, Full of Action Movie Clichés

Sections in Screenwriting Unchained

- 'Characterisation' in 2.3 Craft the Draft
- 3.0 Developing a Character-Led Story
- 4.0 Developing a Theme-Led story
- 6.2 Story Design Tools

Sections in 12 Ways to a Stronger Screenplay

- Character (Change, Growth or Steadfast?)
- Antagonist or Catalyst: Who Is Testing Your Protagonist?

14 The Characters' Backstories Are Irrelevant / Pointless

For a reader or for the audience to notice irrelevant or pointless backstories, this probably means there is too much exposition in the screenplay, so you might first want to take a look at this in 30 The Script Contains Too Much Exposition.

Exposition simply means information, usually related to past events. These events might be relevant to the story, in which case we do need to learn about them, or they might be irrelevant, in which case the writer doesn't need to share them.

For example, past events might be important when it comes to defining who a character is or the decisions they make, but we don't necessarily need to find out about these events. They form the backstory of a character rather than being an integral part of the story itself.

Let's say that our protagonist's father left when they were five. This will clearly impact on who they are, how they form relationships, what they try to achieve in life and why, but depending on the story, the reader / audience might not need to find out about this.

Similarly, the antagonist might have had an affair with the protagonist's partner in the past. This, most likely, would be an element of backstory that we would want to bring to the front at some point, especially if the protagonist isn't aware of it. It could create a feeling of betrayal and shock and would help test the protagonist, as well as reveal a lot about them, depending on their reaction to the news.

But even this part of the backstory of two of the characters (the antagonist and the protagonist's partner) would be irrelevant if revealing it didn't create an interesting twist in the story.

Another possible reason for this note: Some writers believe they have to write a full backstory for each character, including where they were born, what they eat for breakfast, where they went to school, what they look like, etc. While some of this information can be useful and even crucial for some characters, there's no need to fill pages of backstory for all characters. This is a bit like underlining everything in a text: It's as if you hadn't underlined anything.

If writers then share all this mostly random – hence irrelevant – information with the audience, they over-expose their homework and end up with pointless backstories, often conveyed through dialogue.

Solutions

To avoid this, here are a few tips:

✓ **When you design your characters, try to think about a primary characteristic** that will give you a clear handle on them (jealous, adventurous, gluttonous, miserly, hedonistic, etc). This defining characteristic will create an archetype, a one-note character.

✓ **Then find a few secondary characteristics**, relevant to this character, in this story, so that they become more complex, more unique than a simple archetype.

✓ **Define any element of backstory that will explain / justify who you want your characters to be, and in which way they might need to evolve.** Why are they so jealous? So insecure? Why do they feel the need to have so many one-night stands? Why are they so shy? That way, the backstory will be relevant because it will give a foundation to your characters and their evolution in the story.

✓ **Of course, you can do it the other way around** – come up with the backstory first and then see in which way this past might nurture character traits that you can use in the story. This should also give the characters a clear function and logical behaviour and evolution.

✓ Irrespective of the way you design your characters, **don't feel the need to tell us about their backstory unless a specific event is key to understanding both the story and**

the character, or creates an interesting plot point (surprise, conflict, dilemma, etc). The work you've put in to design your characters (consciously or not) doesn't need to be conveyed through exposition, for example through the amount of backstory that you share with the audience. If, however, the audience needs to catch up in order to understand the characters, their decisions and evolutions, by all means share this information in the most palatable way possible (usually using conflict or humour to disguise the exposition).

If you'd like to see how it's done, *Silver Linings Playbook* is a masterclass in exposition. The first fifteen minutes tell us all we need to know about Pat's backstory in a funny, conflictual, visual and entertaining way. After that, we're able to identify with him and understand his decisions, his mistakes and his evolution. Past this point, most of the exposition is not related to Pat but to Tiffany (who is a co-protagonist and a catalyst).

✓ **Remember to think about characters in a dynamic way.** Important characters (not only the protagonist) usually evolve in some way over the course of the story. Whether the protagonist needs to grow, as they often do in a plot-led story, or to change, as is the case in a character-led story, think about the evolution of your character. Try setting out a map for this evolution, a few psychological or emotional steps that will cause growth or change in your character (or might lead to a failure to change in a tragic story).

Usually, this need to change or grow is rooted in the character's past, but you can be selective about which key elements from the past you need to convey to the audience. What we're most interested in are the events, usually conflictual, that lead the character to evolve during the story. If past events in your character's backstory are connected to who they are in the present or how they need to grow or change, or how this evolution is made possible, it will help to make your backstory relevant and useful.

✓ **If the backstory is really important, you might want to consider a flashback structure** to limit the amount of exposition. This is what is done in *The Secret in Their Eyes*,

Citizen Kane, Amadeus, True Detective or *Saving Mr. Banks*. In these examples (and many others), the backstory is more important than the present time story. It's essential to our understanding of the characters, their evolution (*Saving Mr. Banks*, which is all about the protagonist coming to terms with her inability to save her father in the past) or failure to change (*Citizen Kane*, which is about Kane's inability to overcome the childhood trauma that made him unable to trust and love others).

Connected Problems in This Book

- 13 The Characters Are Stereotypes or Clichés
- 12 The Characters Are Too Similar
- 05 The Characters Are Flat, Two-Dimensional
- 12 The Characters Are Too Similar
- 06 The Character Logic Is Fuzzy
- 30 The Script Contains Too Much Exposition

Sections in Screenwriting Unchained

- 'Characterisation' and 'Flashbacks: To FB or Not to FB?' in 2.3 Craft the Draft
- 3.0 Developing a Character-Led Story
- 6.2 Story Design Tools

Sections in 12 Ways to a Stronger Screenplay

- Character (Change, Growth or Steadfast?)

15 The Dialogue Is Cheesy, Full of Action Movie Clichés

Here are a few examples of cheesy, action movie dialogue clichés:
"I was born ready"
"We've got company"
"You've got to be kidding me"
"You and what army?"
"I have a bad feeling about this"
"That went well…"
We don't really don't want to see these lines in a script. You might think they help your script fit a specific genre or tone, but they are more likely to suggest complacency or lack of originality to the reader.

Unless you're being tongue-in-cheek with the cliché. In this case, make it clear that you know it's a cliché, that the audience knows it's a cliché, and that for some reason using it is better than coming up with something more original.

If you're writing a first draft, you might use these as space holders until you find something better, but really you want them out as soon as possible. Ideally, try not to write them in the first place.

Instead, you want to come up with memorable lines that will be linked to an original film and will contribute to making it unforgettable:

"I'll be back" and "Hasta la vista, baby" —*The Terminator* and *Terminator 2: Judgment Day*
"Do I feel lucky? Well, do ya, punk?" —*Dirty Harry*
"Why so serious?" —*The Dark Knight*
"I'll make him an offer he can't refuse" —*The Godfather*

What makes these lines different? Didn't they become clichés? Well, first of all, they weren't clichés when they were first written.

They became memorable, often an instant way to reference the films they come from, but they didn't become clichés. In fact, these lines were very distinctive so it's hard to re-use them unless you want to make a direct reference to – or a parody of – the original.

Most importantly, these lines pay off a situation, a character, even the evolution of a relationship (or, for the last one, plant a visual pay-off: The bloody horse's head in Woltz's bed is the reason the line became unforgettable in *The Godfather*; it has little value by itself). They are not lines that are likely to be used for any character, in any situation, and that's one of the reasons why, beyond the economy of words, they became so memorable.

Solutions

To sum it up, if you want to create memorable lines in your screenplays, here are a few tips:

✓ **Avoid dialogue clichés at all costs.** If you're not certain, google "checklists for cheesy dialogue" and make sure your script – irrespective of its genre – doesn't include any of the usual suspects. Or put a questionable line in the search bar and see if it comes up with examples showing it's already been used.

✓ **Focus on the character,** and make the line a pay-off for that character, a line that only that character could say, that could only be said about that character, or is funny because it's that character ("That's very you"—*Terminator 2*)

✓ **Focus on the situation,** and make the line a funny or effective line because it's ironic, or it's an understatement, but it's closely linked to a specific situation in the film ("You're gonna need a bigger boat"—*Jaws)*

✓ **Make'em short.** Great lines of dialogue tend to be short for three reasons. First, short lines are more impactful. Second, they are easier to memorise for the audience, which is how they become part of pop culture. Third, they are more impressive: encapsulating meaning or emotion in just a few words requires talent and is especially rewarding when it leads the audience to fill the gap ("Yes, considerably." —

Casino Royale, Bond's answer to Dryden, his second kill, shooting him as he's saying "The second one is [easier]").

✓ **Pick your moment,** depending on the genre and tone of the story. A witty one-liner can make the audience smile or laugh if it's the right time to release tension, but it can also break the tension or suspense if your timing is wrong. This can be enough for a line to fall flat if it undermines the desired emotion.

✓ **Think visual storytelling and pay-off:** As in the *Casino Royale* example above, a good line of dialogue in an action movie usually pays off a previous scene or situation, and often goes with a visual storytelling moment. It has little value in and by itself. If someone hasn't seen the film, you'd need to explain the set-up and the visual pay-off to make it work ("I'm having an old friend for dinner — *The Silence of the Lambs*").

✓ **Craft running gags and punchlines.** In comedies, a memorable line of dialogue can be a one-off "Toodle-oo, motherfu*ker" — *The Hangover*) or a running gag ("We were on a break!" —*Friends*). In an action movie, a punchline is often planted to pay-off during the climax, when the antagonist is defeated and usually dispatched in style. This is an expected convention.
You can either follow the convention ("Yippee-ki-yay, motherfu*ker" —*Die Hard*, where the punchline is planted when Hans Gruber compares John McClane to a cowboy earlier), or turn it around ("You either die a hero, or live long enough to become a villain" —*The Dark Knight*, where this earlier line of dialogue plants a less conventional ending, as Harvey Dent is a more complex character than Hans Gruber).

All of this should help you avoid cheesy, action movie cliché dialogue, and hopefully say "Hasta la vista, baby!" to this note.

Connected Problems in This Book

- 37 The Protagonist Is a Conventional Hero

Sections in Screenwriting Unchained

- 'Visual Storytelling' and 'Planting and Pay-Off' in 2.1 Behind the Scenes

Sections in 12 Ways to a Stronger Screenplay

- Planting, Pay-Off and Visual Storytelling

16 The Scenes Are Aimless, There Is No Dramatic Conflict

Writers are more likely to get this note when they haven't fully grasped the fractal aspect of story structure. When you think about the three-act structure in terms of number of pages or minutes – I call this the *logistical* three-act structure – then it can only apply to the whole story. It's a superficial way to define, rather than design, a story. More importantly, it most often misses the actual *dramatic* structure of the script. It's about story format, not story structure.

If you think about the three-act structure in a dramatic way, i.e. before, during and after a main dramatic action or evolution, then you can use the same tool to design the story as a whole, but also its parts: dramatic scenes, sequences, acts, subplots or strands...

This fractal aspect of story structure is a key part of the Story-Type Method. I develop this in great detail in *Screenwriting Unchained*, with many info-graphs to help visualise this in the introduction and first chapter, so I'll keep it brief here. Please see If You Want to Find Out More... at the end of this book for a download link to a free sampler that will cover this.

Think about the main problem in each scene, and who is trying to resolve it

Improving the dramatic structure of each scene is key to addressing this note. The protagonist of the film tends to be the protagonist of most sequences and scenes, but occasionally it will be another character (or group of characters) who will be the protagonist of a scene.

Once you've decided *who wants what and why* in the scene, you have your protagonist and your goal for the scene. You can then handle this scene as a mini-movie, making sure the audience understands what's at stake. As soon as *we* understand who wants what and why, we enter dramatic Act 2 of the scene. Many scenes don't have a first dramatic act, simply because we have defined the protagonist's goal at the end of an earlier scene, so when the scene starts we already know what's at stake.

Once you give an answer to the dramatic question in the scene (Will the protagonist reach the goal or not?) during the climax of the scene, we enter dramatic Act 3, which shows the consequences of the protagonist's action. Having tried to achieve something during the scene, and having either succeeded or failed, what is the protagonist going to do next? It's also an opportunity to explore emotions: how is the success or failure of the protagonist in the scene going to impact on them and the other characters?

Make sure that most scenes are connected to the main plot (or theme)

Identifying the story-type of your project will help you to focus on the backbone of your story. By the way, don't worry if you struggle to follow what I'm attempting to summarise below in just a few paragraphs. It may need more explanation, diagrams, exercises, details and examples to make complete sense. If so, you can explore the references provided at the end of the section and dig further.

In a **plot-led story** (where the main problem lies outside of the protagonist), it's usually fairly simple. For example, let's say the protagonist wants to rescue her son who is in trouble (main goal). In order to achieve this, she first has to escape from jail (a subgoal defining a dramatic sequence, which is a number of scenes connected to the same dramatic action).

The first scene of this first dramatic sequence could be to get a cell key from the guard. This is the goal of the scene. If the protagonist gets the key at the end of the scene, you have a positive answer to the dramatic question of the scene. If the protagonist fails to get the key, you have a negative answer and the protagonist needs to either find a new way to get the key, or to find another way out. The outcome of the first scene triggers the next scene: if she's got the key, she tries to use it to escape from her cell. If she hasn't, she starts digging a tunnel.

Once she's out of jail (end of the first sequence), she might have to locate her son. That becomes your second dramatic sequence. And so on...

If you make sure that each scene starts, develops or closes a dramatic sequence, you'll seriously reduce your chances of getting this note because the audience will be able to connect what's at stake in the scene (getting a cell key) to what's at stake in the sequence (getting out of jail) to what's at stake in the film (rescuing her son). Your scenes won't be aimless, and provided the protagonist comes across obstacles on the sub-subgoals (scene level), subgoals (sequence level) and goal (story level), there will also be dramatic conflict.

This conflict can come from antagonistic characters or forces, but it can also come from an internal obstacle that makes it more difficult for the protagonist to reach the goal. For example, our prisoner could be non-violent, so would not consider using force to reach her goal / subgoal.

You could also have a character-led subplot: while the story is plot-led (the main problem lies outside the protagonist, in our example let's say it's the antagonist threatening her son's life), there could be a need to grow in order to reach the goal and some of your scenes could explore that part of the story rather than the main plot.

For example, our protagonist loves her son but they have a difficult relationship due to a past event or an internal flaw that the protagonist needs to resolve. The protagonist will have to grow to succeed. This psychological / emotional part of the story isn't the main plot, it's not the main problem, it's just a character-led element that makes the character – hence the story – more interesting. Some scenes will explore this, but most scenes will be about the main, external problem.

In a **character-led story** (where the main problem lies within the protagonist), it becomes more complex because although the protagonist can have a conscious goal and explore different ways to reach it, what's really at stake is their unconscious need to change. The main problem in the story isn't external, it's internal. This means that most of the conflict in each scene comes from the protagonist themselves. The protagonist *is* the antagonist.

In such stories, characters who look like antagonists on the conscious goal are in fact co-protagonists on the unconscious need: They cause conflict that forces the protagonist to change. For example, in *Silver Linings Playbook*, Tiffany isn't an antagonist, even if she's the source of most of the external conflict in the story for our protagonist, Pat. She is a catalyst, a character who forces (helps) Pat to change.

In character-led stories, you have to design most scenes so that the conflict generated is a step towards the protagonist's change. Dramatic sequences aren't designed as subgoals to reach a main conscious goal, they are designed so that through trying to achieve something consciously, the protagonist is going to experience the conflict that is going to lead them to change, one psychological / emotional step at a time.

When you design each scene, you have to see it both in the context of the conscious goal (what the character wants in the film and in the scene) but also in the context of what the character needs, which is to change. In *Silver Linings Playbook*, Pat *wants* to get back with his wife Nikki. That's his conscious goal. But what he *needs* is to let go of her so he can be happy with Tiffany. It makes each scene more complex to write, because you have to deal with these two levels, but it also makes the scenes very rewarding.

Define what stands in the way of your protagonist, because this is how you'll generate dramatic conflict

In **plot-led stories**, this will tend to be external obstacles (antagonistic characters or forces, such as nature in a disaster movie), although you can still use internal obstacles (character traits that make it more difficult for the protagonist to reach their goal, as explained above).

In **character-led stories**, the antagonist will be the protagonist themselves, although you will often have a catalyst character, a character who looks like an antagonist on the conscious goal but who is in fact forcing / helping the protagonist to change (hence a co-protagonist on the unconscious need).

It becomes more complex if you're dealing with a **theme-led story** (multi-stranded narrative where the main problem usually lies in society) because you have to handle different strands and connect each scene not only to the scenes in the same strands but also ideally to other strands. Either way, each scene should explore the same theme, as this is what ties your story together. Thanks to the fractal aspect of story structure, each strand can be structured like a mini-movie: identify what's at stake in the strand, and handle it with a dramatic three-act structure: before, during and after the main dramatic action or evolution. Then sequence each strand as if it was a plot-led or a character-led story, following the above suggestions.

Keep in mind that managing conflict (who wants / needs what and why) is only one side of structure

Managing information (who knows what when) is an equally important part, often more important in hybrids and exceptions. This is true at film level, but it's also true at sequence or scene level.

For example, you could decide to structure a scene or a whole dramatic sequence not over a dramatic action / subgoal, but over a dramatic irony (the audience knows something that at least one character isn't aware of).   Instead of wondering "Will the protagonist reach the goal?" the audience will want to see how and when the victim of the dramatic irony (the character who doesn't know) will find out. This moment is called the resolution of the dramatic irony. In a way, the audience gives the victim the unconscious goal of finding out what they know and the victim doesn't.

Each scene in such a sequence would exploit the dramatic irony: make the most of the situation, even if the victim doesn't have a strong conscious goal.

This is another powerful way to generate conflict and give a clear direction to a scene or a sequence. It's used to generate suspense in a thriller (we know that the man Clarice is questioning at the end of *The Silence of the Lambs* is the serial killer she's been trying to catch, she doesn't) or humour in a comedy (we know that Michael Dorsey is a man pretending to be a woman in *Tootsie*, most of the other characters don't).

As you can see, structure is more than a logistical, superficial three-act format over the whole script, and it's just the same at scene level. But if you're careful to 1) define who wants / needs what and why in each scene as well as what stands in the way and 2) keep in mind who knows what when, making sure that the conflict you are generating in the scene is relevant to the overall problem (reaching a conscious goal, resolving an unconscious need), then you should significantly reduce the odds of ever seeing this note again.

If, following the same principles, you also use dramatic sequences to break down the main dramatic action or evolution, it will make it easier for the audience to follow the story and get emotionally involved in each scene.

I dedicate a whole section in *Screenwriting Unchained* to scene writing because it's such an essential aspect of the craft. Mastering dramatic tools at scene level is easier than at sequence or script level, so it's a fantastic way to learn and practice. It's also the best way to write a great screenplay: one well-structured scene at a time. So if you'd like to explore this further, you know where to look!

Solutions

Let's sum it up in a few actionable tips:

✓   **Does your scene have a clear protagonist?** Remember, the protagonist is the character who experiences the most conflict. Look at who wants / needs what and why in the scene. This will help you give a direction to the scene, and – if something or someone stands in the way of the protagonist – a way to create dramatic conflict in the scene.

✓   **Is your scene connected to the main dramatic action** (for example it's part of a dramatic sequence that explores a subgoal, a way for the protagonist to reach the goal) **or the main dramatic evolution** (it causes some conflict for the protagonist and contributes to a character change or explores a dilemma)?

✓   **Is your scene connected to a subplot?** This is a problem less important than the main problem in the story, but connected to it. Often, the protagonist of a subplot isn't the protagonist of the main plot. Make sure that you don't spend too much time lost in a subplot.

✓   **In a theme-led story, is your scene connected to the main theme?** This is essential, but don't forget to design it with a protagonist in order to generate conflict, emotion and give a dramatic direction to the scene.

✓   **Is there enough causality (cause and effect) in the scenes?** Is each scene caused by what has happened before, and does it cause further events in the story? Or can you take scenes out, without causing any issue? Can you swap two scenes easily? This usually means that there isn't enough causality in the story and might lead to this note. More on this in 25 The Narrative Is Episodic or Repetitive.

✓   **If a scene can't be designed around a main dramatic question, can it be designed around a main ironic question?** Instead of wondering: Will the protagonist reach the goal? the audience might be wondering: How and when will the victim of a dramatic irony find out what we know and they don't, and how will they react?

✓   **Not all scenes need to have a strong dramatic structure, but they all need to have a purpose,** and ideally to achieve more than one thing at once. Does each scene move the action forward, tell us something about the characters or explore the theme in some way? Does it set-up, exploit or resolve a dramatic irony, play with a mystery or deliver a surprise? All these elements can be used to give direction to your scenes and fill them with dramatic conflict.

Connected Problems in This Book

- 29 The Plot Is Slowed Down By Unconnected Storylines
- 31 The Drama / Conflict Is Told But Not Shown
- 20 The Conflict Is Artificial or Inconsequential
- 25 The Narrative Is Episodic or Repetitive

Sections in Screenwriting Unchained

- 1.1 What's Wrong with the Three-Act Structure?
- 2.1 Behind the Scenes

Sections in 12 Ways to a Stronger Screenplay:

- Fractal Aspect of Story Structure

17 The Script Loses the Plot in the Third Act

What many people in the industry call the "third act" is the last twenty-five percent of the story, so the last thirty minutes in a two-hour film. Usually you'll get this note if, in the last half-hour or so, we lose track of who wants what and why and are unable to figure out what's at stake in the story. Or you might have started to explore a new dramatic question in that part of the story (different protagonist, different goal) that bears little connection to what happened before or doesn't answer the dramatic question(s) you raised at the beginning.

There are many ways to structure the last thirty minutes of a screenplay, but the first thing to do is to make the distinction between logistical acts and dramatic acts. Although I'll do my best to convey the gist of it in this section, I cover this in detail in the introduction and first chapter of *Screenwriting Unchained*. You'll find a link to a free sampler of the book (first fifty pages) in the last section, If You Want to Find Out More...

This note is logistical rather than structural. It simply means that the script becomes confusing in logistical Act III (the last twenty-five to thirty minutes of the film). It points to a symptom, not a problem.

Overall, the best way to avoid this note is to have a strong grasp on the dramatic engine of your project, hence to be clear about its story-type.

In a plot-led story (where the main problem lies outside the protagonist), the structure is shaped around a main dramatic *action* (who *wants* what and why). If the story is classically structured, we have three dramatic acts because we have what happens before, during and after this main dramatic action. The climax answers the main dramatic question, which is "Will the protagonist reach their conscious goal or not?" This defines what's primarily at stake in the story. Usually, this question isn't answered until the very end of the film (in the last ten minutes or so). You'll often get this note if you've answered the dramatic question too early, hence have a dramatic Act 3 that's too long, or if it becomes unclear what the dramatic question is. In most modern plot-led stories, the protagonist needs to grow, but rarely to change. Their evolution defines a character-led subplot, not the main plot. If this character evolution takes over towards the end of the story, you're likely to confuse the reader regarding what's primarily at stake.

In a character-led story (where the main problem lies within the protagonist), the structure is shaped around the main dramatic *evolution* of the protagonist (who *needs* what and why). If it's classically structured, we have three dramatic acts because we have what happens before, during and after this main dramatic evolution. The climax answers the main dramatic question, which is "Will the protagonist find a way to change or not?" This is what's primarily at stake in the story, and this question remains unanswered until the very end. Often, character-led stories are disguised as plot-led, to make them more accessible and to widen their potential audience. For example, *Little Miss Sunshine* looks like it's about getting Olive to the pageant in time, when it's in fact about the whole family becoming less dysfunctional. Either way, if you lose track of what's really at stake in your story, so will the audience and you'll end up with this note. It will also make it more difficult to find a satisfying ending.

In a theme-led story (a multi-stranded narrative where the main problem usually lies in society), there is no main dramatic action or evolution because the story has only subplots and no main plot. If readers are confused towards the end of the story, it might be because you have lost sight of the theme connecting all the various strands, or it might become apparent that the strands are not connected anymore, or you might have started exploring a new theme. Or perhaps you've suddenly focused on one strand and forgotten the others. In a multi-stranded narrative, we don't have a dramatic three-act structure but a thematic one: before we understand the theme, while we explore it, and the consequences of this exploration. This unique theme defines the backbone of your story. Lose sight of it, fail to define it precisely, and the last part of the story might well fall apart.

In a hybrid or exception (we can't identify a main problem or there is more than one), this can be more difficult to diagnose, but you could be getting this note because you forgot to exploit or resolve the main dramatic irony (something that the audience knows but at least one character, the victim of the irony, isn't aware of) that might have been shaping the story up to that point. Or your non-linear narrative or flashback structure might have become too difficult to follow. In that case, check that you actually need the unconventional structure, and that the story is clear and complex, not just confusing. More on this in 35 The Script Is Unnecessarily Complex.

Solutions

Let's recap the main potential problems behind this note and what can be done to resolve them:

✓   In the last third of your script, **the protagonist has a new goal** that isn't related to the main goal (not a consequence, not logically connected, not a subgoal), or no longer has a goal.

In that case, make sure that whatever the protagonist is trying to achieve at this point in the story is connected to the main dramatic action or evolution.

For example, in a plot-led story, the protagonist should be exploring one last way to reach the main goal. This subgoal defines a last dramatic sequence before the climax, during which the protagonist should be facing the strongest external obstacles, possibly an internal obstacle as well, if that hasn't been resolved previously.

In a character-led story, this last sequence should be the final push, the last conflict or dilemma that's going to confirm the protagonist's change or their failure to evolve.

In any case, verify that the climax towards the very end of the story answers the main dramatic question: Does the protagonist reach their goal (plot-led story)? Does the protagonist find a way to change, to move on (character-led story)?

✓ In the last third of your script, **we're confused by what's at stake**.

We thought we were watching a character-led story, so we thought the stakes were centred around the unconscious need for the protagonist to change, but suddenly the story becomes plot-led (the main problem seems external). It becomes about survival, or any other plot-led goal. This is unlikely to work if you haven't prepared the audience for this and developed the story as a hybrid, such as *Edge of Tomorrow*, where such a story-type change from character-led to plot-led takes place earlier in the story.

Similarly, we thought we were watching a plot-led story, and the ending becomes entirely about the need for the character to grow, which can be confusing. This need to grow in a plot-led story is often exploited as a dilemma during the climax. It can also be resolved before the climax in order to give the protagonist a chance to succeed. It can even happen after the climax, to show a consequence of the action and of the conflict experienced by the protagonist during the story. But you need to be clear about the story-type (plot-led or character-led), otherwise you'll send confusing signals about what's at stake during the last part of the story and your chances of getting this note increase astronomically.

Either way, the solution is the same as above: make sure that the climax towards the end of the story answers the main dramatic question.

✓ In the last third of the script, **characters start to behave and make decisions not according to who they are** and what has happened before in the story, but according to how the writer wants the story to end. This will make the ending feel contrived, or will lead to events or decisions that have not been planted sufficiently. In this case, start with the ending that you want, then go back and plant what needs to happen during the story so that final actions or decisions come from the characters reacting to events according to who they are at that stage and not from your own agenda.

✓ **The theme isn't clear enough** (the writer doesn't know, consciously or not, what the story is about, what the main problem is or what their point of view is on this problem), hence they find it difficult to bring the narrative to a close. If you think this might be the case for your project, remember that most of the meaning is conveyed through the ending of the story, so first ask yourself what your point of view is about the main problem. Clarify what the story is about. It should help you to focus and find the right outcome. If this doesn't work, consider redesigning the project as a multi-stranded narrative (theme-led story), especially if the main problem lies in society and it feels artificial and unsatisfying to force a yes / no answer to a complex problem. This will allow you to explore the same problem through different characters / storylines, and to find a different resolution in each strand – some positive, some negative.

✓ **You might be missing a trick regarding managing information (who knows what when).** You forgot to exploit or resolve a dramatic irony set up earlier in the story (the audience knows something that at least one character isn't aware of). Perhaps a final twist isn't believable because it's not been seeded enough previously, or a mystery lasts for too long or is lifted in a convoluted or unconvincing way. All these can result in this note. So look closely at the way you manage information in your story, as it can be part of story structure.

For example, if the flower girl at the end of *City Lights* never realised who the tramp was and what he'd done for her, or if Roxane never found out that Cyrano was the one who wrote the letters and came up with the lines that made her fall in love with Christian, the script would "lose the plot in the third act".

Connected Problems in This Book

- 10 The Ending Doesn't Work
- 34 Too Many Questions Are Left Unanswered
- 22 The Ending Is an Anti-Climax

- 23 The Ending Is a *Deus Ex Machina*
- 08 The Story Is Confusing
- 35 The Script Is Unnecessarily Complex
- 18 There Is No Clear Protagonist
- 24 There Is No Clear Antagonist
- 19 The Script Feels Formulaic
- 25 The Narrative Is Episodic or Repetitive
- 38 The Plot Is Contrived

Sections in Screenwriting Unchained

- 'Happy Ending vs. Satisfying Ending' and 'Encore Twist' in 2.3 Craft the Draft
- 2.0 Developing a Plot-Led Story
- 3.0 Developing a Character-Led Story
- 4.0 Developing a Theme-Led Story
- 5.0 Developing Something Else (Hybrids and Exceptions)

Sections in 12 Ways to a Stronger Screenplay

- Managing Conflict (Who Wants / Needs What and Why?)
- Managing Information (Who Knows What When?)
- Character (Change, Growth or Steadfast?)
- Satisfying Ending

18 There Is No Clear Protagonist

This one isn't necessarily a problem... First see <u>01 We Don't Care About the Protagonist</u> and <u>28 The Protagonist Is Not Strong Enough</u> for a definition of what a protagonist is.

There are some stories where there is no clear protagonist, and that's not a problem if the story is well-designed.

This could be the case in a theme-led story, where we don't have a protagonist because there is no main plot, only subplots called strands. In *Crash, Traffic, Game of Thrones, Friends* or *Magnolia*, there is no clear protagonist because these are well-designed theme-led stories: multi-stranded narratives where the main problem lies in society. In these stories, we identify with more than one protagonist, because each separate strand is usually structured around one dramatic action or evolution, with its own protagonist. Each strand is also connected to at least another strand and they all explore the same theme to give some unity to the overall narrative.

It could also be a story with a protagonist-antagonist structure, where we can identify with either the protagonist or the antagonist (or both). This is how *Heat* is designed. I would say that bank robber Neil McCauley is the protagonist and Detective Vincent Hanna the antagonist, but it's a close call. They both experience a lot of conflict, and depending on who you are and which character you root for most, you can identify with McCauley, Hanna, or both. In this case, as with theme-led stories, there's no clear protagonist and it isn't a problem. Structure is subjective. As long as you can identify with either character, it doesn't matter which one because the ending is written so that it's satisfying from both points of view.

Successful hybrids and exceptions often have no clear protagonist. For example, who is the protagonist of *The Lives of Others*, *Psycho* or *L.A. Confidential*?

So the real challenge is to assess when this note is relevant, and when it's not.

Assuming that this note isn't delivered on dogmatic grounds, the problem isn't that there is no clear protagonist. As we've explained, this isn't necessarily an issue. The *symptom* is that there is no clear protagonist, but the *problem* is that there is no character we can identify with or relate to in the story, and / or that nothing is at stake.

In order to resolve this, the first step is to assess which story-type you're dealing with, and why the reader is unable to identify with any of the characters.

If you're dealing with a **plot-led story** (the main problem lies outside the protagonist) or a **character-led story** (the main problem lies within the protagonist), then take a look at <u>01 We Don't Care About the Protagonist</u>. It should help you to establish why, if you do have a protagonist in your story, it's not clear who they are. In these story-types, not having a clear protagonist is a problem because it prevents us from identifying with any of the characters.

If you're dealing with a **theme-led story** (a multi-stranded narrative where the main problem lies in society), you don't need a clear protagonist over the whole story as there is no main dramatic action or evolution, but you do need a clear protagonist in each strand. Assuming you're following the advice in <u>01 We Don't Care About the Protagonist</u> at strand level, the main reason why we might not care about any of the characters is if what's at stake in each strand is too abstract or if the main problem in each strand is too esoteric. See Is Maslow Running the Show? at the end of the first chapter of *Screenwriting Unchained* for more details.

There is another situation that can trigger this note, which is when you're dealing with co-protagonists: two or more characters sharing the same **conscious goal** – as in *The Magnificent Seven*, *Alien*, *The Heat*, *Bird Box* or *Saving Private Ryan* – or **unconscious need**, as in *Little Miss Sunshine* and many romantic comedies or buddy movies.

In this case, as long as you handle the group of characters as the protagonist of the story, there is no reason to make any single character the main protagonist. You could focus more on one character in the group (say Ripley in *Alien* or Captain John Miller in *Saving Private Ryan*), but that's not mandatory. Each character in the group is designed as an individual, different from the others. But you don't need to have any single character as "the protagonist", because the protagonist is this group of characters sharing the same *want* or *need*.

What you have to assess is whether you do have a protagonist made of a group of characters sharing the same goal (want or need), or if you have no protagonist.

Again, the note is more likely to land on your desk if the script doesn't work. So instead of thinking "I have to have a main protagonist", look at the way you manage conflict and information, and check whether you can improve this so that the audience is able to identify / empathise with at least one character or group of characters sharing the same goal. The way to achieve this is detailed in 01 We Don't Care About the Protagonist.

Solutions

To sum it up, here's how to deal with this note:

✓ **Assess whether the note points to a problem** (because of the way it's designed, you should have a clear protagonist in your story, but don't have one at the moment) **or a symptom** (it's not possible to identify with any character in the story, but this doesn't mean you should have a single, clear protagonist).

✓ **Decide if the note is relevant because your project falls into one of the situations described above, or irrelevant because it's a dogmatic note.** Some people dismiss all the examples above and actually believe that you can't tell a story if it doesn't have a clear protagonist. You need to find a way to argue your case and explain why your story, although unconventionally structured, works (as long as it does), and why defining a clear protagonist will not make it better, just different and possibly worse. Before you have this discussion though, make sure that your story *does* work as an exception. Someone might have come up with the wrong solution, but before rejecting it, check that it wasn't triggered by a real problem.

✓ **This usually comes down to assessing your story-type.** If the story is plot-led or character-led, you tend to need a clear protagonist. In **plot-led stories**, you can also have co-protagonists, a group of characters trying to solve the same external problem. In **character-led stories**, this is less prevalent as we tend to have a single protagonist dealing with an internal problem. But it can happen, as in *Little Miss Sunshine*, where the protagonist is the whole family, and they need as a group to become less dysfunctional. Or in romantic comedies, such as *Silver Linings Playbook*, where we end up caring equally for the two main characters who share the need to up end with each other. Or in buddy movies, where the co-protagonists share the need to become friends and complete each other. In **theme-led stories**, you don't have a clear protagonist as you have potentially one protagonist per strand.

✓ **If your intention *is* to have a clear protagonist**, because you do want the audience to closely identify emotionally with a character, **then make sure that there is a character – or group of characters sharing the same goal – who experience more conflict than the others in the story.** Conflict that we can understand, related to a problem that someone can do something about, consciously or not. This is closely connected to the way you manage conflict and information in the story, as both are linked.

✓ **If you don't want or need to have a clear protagonist in your story**, for example because you're dealing with a **theme-led story**, then make sure that you structure as many strands as possible as plot-led or character-led, so that you do have a clear protagonist in each strand, and check that each strand is connected to the same theme. This should make it possible to identify with more than one character, instead of identifying with none.

✓ **If you're dealing with a hybrid or exception**, as usual you're more or less on your own. Be aware that in order to develop an exception that handles more than one protagonist successfully, you need to know what you're doing in order to make it possible for the audience to identify emotionally with various characters, either simultaneously or successively.

In *Psycho* for example, we start with Marion Crane, then switch to Norman Bates, before switching again to the detective, Arbogast, and finally to Marion's boyfriend and sister.

A similar feat is achieved in *Three Billboards Outside Ebbing, Missouri*, as we start with Mildred Hayes and we end with Dixon. Everything is possible, as long as it works.

However, dealing with more than one protagonist can be hard, both to pull off in the story design and when the time comes to try to get the project green-lit, even when the story works as an exception.

Connected Problems in This Book

- 01 We Don't Care About the Protagonist
- 24 There Is No Clear Antagonist
- 28 The Protagonist Is Not Strong Enough
- 02 We Don't Care About the Story

Sections in Screenwriting Unchained

- 1.1 What's Wrong About the Three-Act Structure?
- 'Protagonist vs Main Character', 'Protagonist vs Antagonist', 'Hero vs Protagonist' in 2.3 Craft the Draft
- 3.3 Grow the Draft
- '*The Intouchables*' and '*Silver Linings Playbook*' in 3.5 Case Studies
- 4.3 Weave the Draft
- '*Crash*' and '*Cloud Atlas*' in 4.4 Case Studies
- 5.1 Story-Types Are Structural Templates, Not Rigid Formulas
- '*The Lives of Others*' and '*L.A. Confidential*' in 5.2 Case Studies

Sections in 12 Ways to a Stronger Screenplay

- Story-Type and Genre

19 The Script Feels Formulaic

This note often lands on a writer's desk when they are following a prescriptive formula, making sure their story hits the mandatory three-acts, eight sequences, fifteen beats, twenty-two steps, etc. Unfortunately, mandatory plot-points only mean predictability, hence boredom.

There is simply no theoretical justification for anything to happen at any specific page number in a screenplay. Are there well-known, long-established dramatic principles? Sure. Tools that all writers would benefit from mastering? Certainly. But particular story beats to integrate into any story at specific times or page numbers? Archetypal characters that should be present in any story, irrespective of its genre (or absence of), even when it has little mythical inspiration? Absolutely not.

Such a thought can be scary to the beginner and even to the seasoned screenwriter, but once you start to look into it, it becomes liberating. Whether it is prescriptive act lengths, number or length of dramatic sequences, presence of a mandatory midpoint, specific location of turning points including inciting incidents or climaxes, all these "rules" come from a fear of risk, a fear of the unknown, rather than sound dramatic principles.

The myth is that the industry loves the idea of formulas, because it suggests that success can be repeated if you follow a simple recipe. The truth is, especially in a spec script, producers and development execs all want the same thing: an original voice in a story that works. No one cares about the way it works if it makes the reader turn the pages because they're hooked. And blindly embracing a supposed paradigm, whatever it is, is almost guaranteed to lead to the exact opposite reaction.

Of course, there is no reason you can't use the logistical tools or formulas if they help your productivity, just so long as you don't take them as gospel and understand that the underlying structure in a good story is far more complex, flexible and unpredictable.

Remember, you're free to do anything you want, as long as it works.

There is only one rule: "Thou shalt not be boring".

Solutions

So how do we address this note?

✓ **Throw away any prescriptive screenwriting book that tells you what you have to do and when,** those that set mandatory steps or plot points, any number of acts or sequences, and insist that every story should follow the same paradigm or hit the same beats. These are about story format, not story structure. Once you've ditched formulaic theories, focus on structural elements that help you design a story in a more organic, unpredictable, original way.

✓ **Study how managing conflict (Who wants / needs what and why?) really works,** taking in the difference between a hero and a protagonist or between an antagonist and a villain. Realising that we empathise with the character who experiences the most conflict, not the character who is the nicest conceptually, or who changes most, is a first step in the right direction.

It leads us to the idea that in character-led stories, where the main problem lies within the protagonist, there is no antagonist. This is because the protagonist, fighting their internal flaw, *is* the antagonist, the main source of conflict for the protagonist. Antagonistic characters in a character-led story are often catalysts, characters who force the protagonist to change, helping them reach their unconscious need. This is explored in detail in *Screenwriting Unchained* and you'll find a summary in 01 We Don't Care About the Protagonist and 02 We Don't Care About the Story.

✓ **Discover how managing information (Who knows what when?) is as much part of story structure as managing conflict.** Dramatic irony (the audience knows something that at least one character is unaware of) can be the main structural tool used to design successful comedies such as *Tootsie* or *There's Something About Mary*. It's also a classic tool used to generate suspense in thrillers, as in *Misery*, *The Hand that Rocks the Cradle* or *Bird Box*. In these films, the audience knows where the threat is coming from before the protagonist does, which creates a lot of conflict and helps with identification. Mastering dramatic irony will have a far bigger impact on your writing, irrespective of the genre or tone of your story, than following any prescriptive formula. Many hybrids and exceptions, such as *The Lives or Others* or *The Departed*, use managing information and especially dramatic irony to create an unusual yet compelling story. This is also developed extensively in *Screenwriting Unchained*, but you can find an overview in <u>04 The Story Is Linear, Feels Predictable</u>.

Connected Problems in This Book:
- 01 We Don't Care About the Protagonist
- 02 We Don't Care About the Story
- 37 The Protagonist Is a Conventional Hero
- 26 The Villains or Antagonists Are Weak or Unconvincing
- 04 The Story Is Linear, Feels Predictable
- 13 The Characters Are Stereotypes or Clichés
- 15 The Dialogue Is Cheesy, Full of Action Movie Clichés

Sections in Screenwriting Unchained:
- 1.1 What's Wrong with the Three-Act Structure?
- 2.0 Developing a Plot-Led Story
- 3.0 Developing a Character-Led Story
- 4.0 Developing a Theme-Led Story
- 5.0 Developing Something Else: Hybrids and Exception
- 5.1 Story-Types Are Structural Templates, Not Rigid Formulas

Sections in 12 Ways to a Stronger Screenplay:
- Story-Type and Genre

- Theme (What Is the Story About?)
- Satisfying Ending

20 The Conflict Is Artificial or Inconsequential

This note often stems from the way conflict in a screenplay is defined and understood. The focus tends to be on characters opposing each other in scenes where they fight or argue endlessly, simply to add more conflict to the story. I could just as easily have called this section "The Characters Are Yelling at Each Other for No Reason."

Or the conflict, when more subtle, isn't sufficiently connected to the rest of the story. It doesn't stem from what has happened before, and doesn't lead to anything.

Or, more importantly, the conflict doesn't lead to any emotion or evolution.

While it's true that conflict is important and that a dramatic story without conflict is likely to be boring, we need to understand why we need conflict, how we can generate it in more subtle ways than having characters shouting or throwing punches at each other and how we can make sure it's connected to the rest of the story.

Why do we need conflict?

There are quite a few reasons for having conflict in a dramatic story.

1) It makes the story more believable: There is a lot of conflict in life, so putting some in our stories make them more life-like, which means it's easier to suspend our disbelief.

2) It generates interest: Conflictual situations often grab attention more easily than non-conflictual ones (hence why the news is mostly made of bad news, not good news).

3) It also generates identification, because the protagonist in a story is the character (or group of characters sharing the same goal) who experiences the most conflict in the story.

But there are two even more important reasons why we need conflict in a story...

4) Conflict leads to emotion, which is what we're after when we watch a film. Whether it's drama, excitement, terror, laughter, we're looking for emotion. If there is no conflict, there is no emotion and the story becomes cold and dull. There is a great scene illustrating this link between conflict and emotion in *Birdman*. Riggan discovers that his daughter Sam, whom he's hired as a personal assistant to help her to stop taking drugs, is smoking pot. They argue, so the scene is full of conflict, but it leads to intense emotions, both for them and, through identification, the audience. Sam tells hard truths that are painful for Riggan to hear, especially coming from his own daughter. Some of what she says is true, and it hurts. So we feel for him. But she also realises that she's gone too far. She regrets it, but there's nothing she can do, so we feel for her too. Although there was conflict to start with, the scene ends on the emotion, for the characters and for the audience. This is the first thing you want to check in your story: it's great to have conflict, but does this conflict lead to emotion, for the characters and more importantly for the audience?

5) Conflict also leads to evolution (growth or change), which is often what gives depth to the characters, makes them more interesting, makes us care for them because they behave like us: human beings resisting change because it's painful, sometimes forced to change by the conflict they experience. This is often true in life, and this is how it works in a story.

Solutions

How do we generate conflict?

The problem with the simplistic approach of putting a protagonist in a tree and throwing rocks at them is that it focuses on external conflict. Internal conflict is often more subtle because it relies on our knowledge of the internal flaw a character is fighting against, whether it is shyness or clumsiness in a comedy (Ted in

There's Something About Mary), fear of water in a sea-based thriller (Chief Brody in *Jaws*) or soul-destroying jealousy (Salieri in *Amadeus*). This immediately generates situations that are more subtle and rewarding than simply having people fighting with each other (which does also happen in these films, it's just not the sole way to generate conflict).

So, let's look at managing information, which is deeply connected to managing conflict. If, instead of having characters in direct opposition all the time, we think about the information we could communicate to the audience so that we know about a danger, a problem, but at least some of the characters don't, we can generate a lot of conflict without any apparent opposition between the characters in the film. This is what Hitchcock describes as "the bomb under the table" in a thriller, and what we'll call dramatic irony. For example, in *The Apartment*. When C.C. Baxter lends his key to his boss without knowing that his boss is taking the woman Baxter loves to his apartment, there is no apparent conflict between the characters, but it "feels" intensely conflictual. This is purely due to the way Wilder and I.A.L. Diamond manage information.

Looking into managing information (Who knows what when?) as well as managing conflict (Who wants / needs what and why?) is going to help generate a wider variety of conflict, and ideally conflict that is connected to the rest of the story, which leads us to the next point.

How do we connect conflict to the rest of the story so that it doesn't feel artificial?

Ideally, you want to generate conflict that is based on the situation or on the characters, instead of coming up with predictable scares or random gags or jokes. A masterful horror or thriller isn't a succession of scary moments. A good comedy isn't a collection of unconnected jokes or gags. A great action film isn't just a string of car chases and set pieces. The scenes are connected to each other and part of a whole.

To achieve this, you need to look at the amount of causality (cause and effect) in your story: do events stem from what happened previously? Do they have consequences later? Does each scene move the plot and / or the characters forward?

A good way to check for causality is to try to take an element out (a character, scene or subplot) and see if the story still makes sense. If it does, there isn't enough causality in the story. You need either to take that element out entirely as you don't need it, or make it impossible to take it out without causing issues in the story logic.

How do we address this according to story-type?

In a **plot-led story** (where the main problem lies outside the protagonist), ensure that beyond the main goal of your protagonist you have defined subgoals (ways for the protagonist to reach the goal). This will help you to design dramatic sequences so that the reader or audience always knows what's at stake over the **whole story** (stealing the money, rescuing the princess, protecting the family, etc) but also in each **sequence** (getting a map of the bank, reaching the top of the tower, locating a shelter) and in as many **scenes** as possible (breaking into the safe, fighting the dragon, crossing the river).

From global to local, if you define dramatic actions at story, sequence and scene level, conflict in a scene will be connected to a dramatic sequence, which will be connected to the overall conscious goal. So no scene, no conflict, should feel inconsequential. If you make sure that this conflict, connected to a wider goal, also causes the evolution of the characters, then you will add another layer. And if each conflict leads to an emotion, for the characters but also for the audience, none of it will feel artificial.

In a character-led story (where the main problem lies within the protagonist), make sure that you have defined the main evolution of your protagonist, as this should be the backbone of the story, not the plot. This makes it possible to have dramatic sequences that are not necessarily connected to the same conscious goal, provided they move the main evolution forward.

So for example in *Groundhog Day*, Phil Connors first tries to get out of the situation, then he tries to make the most of it in a negative way, then he tries to make the most of it in a positive way. This is because what's at stake in the story isn't primarily "Will Phil Connors get what he wants?" (find a way to deal with the situation) but "Will Phil Connors get what he needs?" (become a better person).

This is the same in *As Good As It Gets*, *Silver Linings Playbook*, *Little Miss Sunshine* and *Two Days, One Night*. In all these character-led stories, it's the evolution, not the plot, that shapes the story. So whether the conscious goal remains the same over the whole film (as in *Silver Linings Playbook*, *Two Days, One Night* or *Little Miss Sunshine*) or it keeps changing (*Groundhog Day*), conflict is used as a way to force the protagonist to change, to move on, to get better.

The plot, the conscious goal and the dramatic sequences are there to give the protagonist something to do (dramatic action), so that they experience the conflict that is going to force them to change. If you don't manage conflict that way in a character-led story, it's bound to feel inconsequential or artificial.

In addition, there is always a strong dramatic irony in a character-led story: we know that the protagonist needs to change, and that what they want isn't what they need. Usually, they aren't aware of this, at least to start with. This leads the audience to sense even more conflict for them and strengthens emotional identification.

In a theme-led story (a multi-stranded narrative where the main problem usually lies in society), try to ensure that as many strands as possible are structured as plot-led or character-led, so that you have a clear protagonist and something clearly at stake in each strand, even if there is no clear protagonist over the whole film. This will turn each strand into a mini-movie. Then check that each strand is connected to the same theme, and that the theme is conveyed to the audience as early as possible. This is how stories such as *Crash*, *Magnolia*, *Cloud Atlas*, *Game of Thrones* or *Dunkirk* are designed.

In a hybrid or an exception, you could have different story-types in different parts of the story. *Edge of Tomorrow* (*Live. Die. Repeat.*) is a hybrid that starts as a character-led story and turns into a plot-led one. In that case, deal with each part accordingly. Or you could have a story where the structure is unusual, for example, because it's non-linear (*The Secret in Their Eyes*, *Citizen Kane*, *Memento*) or because it uses dramatic irony as the main structural tool (*The Life of Others*, *The Departed*, *The Hand That Rocks the Cradle*). The key here is to be aware of the structural engine of the story so that you know how to manage conflict and information efficiently, even if it's not done in a conventional way.

Connected Problems in This Book

- 01 We Don't Care About the Protagonist
- 02 We Don't Care About the Story
- 16 The Scenes Are Aimless, There Is No Dramatic Conflict
- 25 The Narrative Is Episodic or Repetitive
- 29 The Plot Is Slowed Down By Unconnected Storylines
- 38 The Plot Is Contrived
- 40 The Premise Is an Artificial Excuse For Action

Sections in Screenwriting Unchained

- 'Managing Conflict', 'Managing Information' and 'Planting and Pay-Off' in 2.1 Behind the Scenes

Sections in 12 Ways to a Stronger Screenplay

- Managing Conflict (Who Want / Needs What and Why?)
- Managing Information (Who Knows What When?)
- Planting, Pay-Off and Visual Storytelling

21 There Is Too Much Dialogue

This note often shows up when there isn't enough design in the story. The lack of dramatic structure forces the writer to deliver too much information through dialogue.

This can also be due to an excess of exposition (characters talking about events instead of the story showing them), but we'll address exposition specifically in 30 The Script Contains Too Much Exposition.

Another reason might be that the writer is trying to write characters that they don't know well enough, or that the writer is writing in a genre they find difficult to handle. If you're good at writing period drama, it might be a stretch to write an action film. If historical sagas are your thing, it might not feel natural to write a hip teenage comedy. The opposite is true: good action or comedy writers might struggle to write more serious drama.

Solutions

So what can we do to address this?

✓ First, **consider structural ways to convey meaning in a story**.

Structure is the combined design of plot, character and theme as well as managing conflict (Who wants / needs what and why?) and managing information (Who knows what when?). The evolution of the characters can also convey meaning.

Do we know what the theme is (What the story is about)? Is the ending satisfying or not? You don't want the characters to explain their intentions or their actions, especially towards the end of the film. You want the audience to understand the meaning of the story from the characters' actions and from the outcome, which is the answer to the dramatic question: Does the protagonist reach the goal in a **plot-led story**? Does the protagonist find a way to change in a **character-led story**? Are all the strands connected to the same theme and do they all contribute to exploring the same problem in society (or in the story world) in a **theme-led story**? What's the answer to the dramatic question in each strand?

✓ Next, **use planting and pay-off for more visual storytelling**.

If you assign a specific meaning to a character, an action, a line of dialogue, an object, a song, you can then achieve visual storytelling when you pay off this element later in the story: the broken mirror in *The Apartment*, the arm of the statue of liberty at the end of *Planet of the Apes*, the sleigh in *Citizen Kane*, the lovers' song in *Casablanca*. This will bring down your reliance on dialogue to convey key pieces of information in the story. It will also help you to make scenes, and especially the ending of your story, more moving and entertaining, as well as meaningful. You'll find much more information about this in the connected problems listed below.

Connected Problems in This Book

- 15 The Dialogue Is Cheesy, Full of Action Movie Clichés
- 09 The Screenplay Is Too Dry or Not Visual Enough
- 30 The Script Contains Too Much Exposition
- 12 The Characters Are Too Similar
- 23 The Ending Is a *Deus Ex Machina*

Sections in Screenwriting Unchained

- 'Visual Storytelling' and 'Planting and Pay-Off' in 2.1 Behind the Scenes
- 'Happy Ending vs. Satisfying Ending' in 2.3 Craft the Draft

Sections in 12 Ways to a Stronger Screenplay

- Planting, Pay-Off and Visual Storytelling
- Satisfying Ending

22 The Ending Is an Anti-Climax

This note comes up fairly often. Here are the three main reasons for it:

1) The ending is expected, predictable, there is no surprise in how we get there.

2) The ending doesn't feel conflictual or emotional enough, there is no suspense around the outcome.

3) The ending leaves some loose ends, for example there is an unresolved mystery. When the audience has spent two hours wondering about a mystery, not getting an answer / solution can be an issue. Some call this an open ending, some call it a frustrating or cryptic ending. Examples: *Caché* (*Hidden*), *Three Billboards Outside Ebbing, Missouri*, *2001: A Space Odyssey*.

Some endings might seem open but are in fact quite clear and non-ambiguous, as in *Thelma & Louise* or *The Big Blue*. We don't wonder what's going to happen to the protagonists. Even if we don't see them actually die, there isn't much doubt about the outcome.

Open endings can work when they allow the audience to make their own interpretation: *Birdman* or *Inception*, for example work for me, but all this is subjective, of course.

Irrespective of personal taste, any audience is likely to be disappointed by a film that ends exactly as we would expect. It doesn't mean that the outcome can't be what the audience wants for the protagonist(s), just that the way to get there should be surprising in some ways.

This usually means playing with the dramatic question right until the end, which is connected to the second possible reason for the note.

In a plot-led story (where the main problem lies outside the protagonist), an ending will feel disappointing if the protagonist overcomes the obstacles – possibly an antagonist – too easily during the climax. This is why we try to get the protagonist to face stronger obstacles as the story unfolds, so that during the climax we're still not sure if the protagonist will succeed.

In a character-led story (where the main problem lies within the protagonist), it will feel unsatisfying if the protagonist changes right at the end, without the audience feeling that this evolution was caused by the conflict experienced by the character during the story, in other words if the evolution isn't a consequence of the action. This is true for the main evolution in a character-led story, but it also applies to a character-led subplot in a plot-led story.

In a theme-led story (a multi-stranded narrative where the main problem usually lies in society), the above applies to each strand as each of them can be plot-led or character-led. The ending itself might feel artificial if all the strands are resolved positively, whether each strand is plot-led or character-led. Or if the point of view of the filmmaker is expressed towards the ending through dialogue, instead of being conveyed through the action and evolution of the characters in each strand.

The ending might also feel like it lacks conflict if a *deus ex machina* concludes the story. We'll look at this special case in 23 The Ending Is a *Deus Ex Machina*.

Solutions

To avoid this problem, you might want to focus on the following:

✓   **Make sure you know what's at stake in your story,** and that the stakes are high during the climax. What happens if the protagonist doesn't reach the goal, or fails to change? You want to have made it clear that this would be catastrophic. If we're not afraid to see the protagonist fail, it's going to be difficult to offer an emotionally rewarding climax to the audience. More on this in 02 We Don't Care About the Story.

✓ **Check that the dramatic question is still open and is still explored during the climax.** Will the protagonist reach the goal or not? Will the protagonist manage to change?

✓ **If a main dramatic irony is shaping your story,** for example if the audience knows that the protagonist is a man when all the characters think he's a woman (*Tootsie*), then **the resolution of the dramatic irony** (when the victims of the dramatic irony find out the truth) **is likely to be part of the climax.** We want to see how all the characters react when they find out what we knew from the beginning. This is true in a comedy (the *Tootsie* example above), a thriller such as *The Hand That Rocks the Cradle* or a drama such as *The Lives of Others*.

✓ **In a plot-led story,** make sure that the protagonist faces the strongest obstacle (or an antagonist at the top of their power) during the climax. If we've seen the protagonist overcome a stronger obstacle earlier, we're unlikely to be hooked when we see them facing a weaker one. If the protagonist has an internal flaw that defines a need to grow, it can be part of the climax as well (Chief Brody having to overcome his fear of water during the climax of *Jaws*), although it's often resolved before (as a way to make the final confrontation possible) or after (the evolution is a consequence of the action).

✓ **In a character-led story,** check that the protagonist is facing their internal demons or the consequences of their lack of evolution, real or perceived, one last time during the climax. Remember that in a character-led story, the protagonist is the antagonist. So if you make it all about a car chase or external obstacles, it's unlikely that the climax will feel satisfying. It should probably be about a dilemma, about a fear, about possibly making the wrong decision. If the protagonist changes, make sure it's because of what happened before in the story, especially the conflict the protagonist has experienced. Each conflict along the way should have caused a step, a minor change towards the overall evolution.

✓ **Verify that you haven't left any unanswered questions, an unresolved mystery, any forgotten subplots,** unless that's truly your intention. This is particularly important in **theme-led stories,** where you have to close all the strands. If you want an open ending, make sure that it's still meaningful and satisfying. An open ending shouldn't be there because you can't decide how to end the story. It should be there because it's the most satisfying ending to the story, and any conclusive ending would be weaker. More on this in <u>34 Too Many Questions Are Left Unanswered</u>.

✓ Sometimes, for example when the main problem lies in society and it's difficult to decide on a positive or a negative ending, you might want to **consider structuring your narrative as a theme-led story.** Problems in society often have no simple solutions, so the ending can feel artificial if it shows a single protagonist resolving the problem. While it might be meaningful for the individual, we know that the wider problem is still there. Exploring the same problem through different storylines in a multi-stranded narrative can be more satisfying because you'll offer a combination of successes and failures, which will illustrate a more complex point of view.

✓ If the ending isn't emotional enough, check that it's a pay-off for the whole story. The most moving endings are planted by what happens before. Instead of dialogue, they often use visual storytelling to pay off such elements. For example, at the end of *City Lights*, the flower girl realises that the man who gave her money to restore her eyesight isn't a generous millionaire, as she thought he was, but a penniless tramp. This pays off the whole story, and it's the visual resolution of a strong dramatic irony (we knew all along that he had no money, she didn't).

Connected Problems in This Book

- 23 The Ending Is a *Deus Ex Machina*
- 34 Too Many Questions Are Left Unanswered
- 19 The Script Feels Formulaic

- 10 The Ending Doesn't Work
- 04 The Story Is Linear, Feels Predictable
- 02 We Don't Care About the Story

Sections in Screenwriting Unchained
- 'Happy Ending vs Satisfying Ending' in 2.3 Craft the Draft

Sections in 12 Ways to a Stronger Screenplay
- Deliver a Satisfying Ending

23 The Ending Is a *Deus Ex Machina*

Let's first define *deus ex machina*.

The expression comes from ancient plays, where the plot was resolved by gods being lowered onto stage on a mechanical platform: "Deus ex machina" – a god from a machine.

This was fairly acceptable in ancient Greece or Rome because the audience believed that various gods were ruling all aspects of their lives.

A few centuries later, it was still acceptable because you had the equivalent of God on Earth: a king or a queen. For example, in Moliere's *Tartuffe*, a messenger from the king arrives at the very end and tells the protagonists that it's fine for them to marry each other even if they are brother and sister, simply because the king says so.

We're less likely to accept this today because we tend to believe that we have more control over our lives and are responsible for our successes and failures. For this reason, a modern audience will tend to reject a solution that doesn't come from the protagonist, or a solution that is too easy for the protagonist to reach, which is exactly what a *deus ex machina* brings.

There is a possible exception to the above, and that's if you're writing for young children. To most young children, parents have an amazing ability to solve problems that seem impossible to overcome. So a young audience might accept a *deus ex machina* in a story more readily, simply because such unplanted, external resolution is part of their lives. It doesn't mean that it's desirable to put a *deus ex machina* in a children's story. You simply might get away with one more easily, especially if the target audience is very young (less than seven years old).

Overall, we have a *deus ex machina* in a story when the protagonist's problem is resolved with external, unplanted help.

For example, let's look at the ending of *Jurassic Park*. The teenage girl's interest in computers is planted early on, but this has little to do with mastering a complex Unix system. So her easy locking of the doors in the control room at the last minute to protect them from the raptors can feel like a *deus ex machina* if you don't enjoy this as a "girl power" moment.

An example of a well-prevented *deus ex machina* can be found in *Gravity*. When Ryan Stone needs to find a way to get to the Chinese station that's about to drift past her, we'd find it hard to swallow if she just spotted a fire extinguisher lying there by chance and had the idea to use it as a jetpack. It would feel too convenient. This is why the presence of the fire extinguisher and the way of using it are planted earlier, during the fire sequence in the Soyuz. Conflict is used to distract the audience (she gets knocked out when she tries to use it to control the fire) and to justify why she takes it with her (it was blocking the hatch). The way a jetpack works is also planted earlier in the film, when Kowalski uses one.

Aliens provides another good example of a well-avoided *deus ex machina*. If, during the climax, Ripley suddenly jumped into a robotic loader that happened to be there and used it as an exoskeleton to fight the alien queen, it would feel very unsatisfying. So these are planted earlier, when the crew uses them to load weapons at the beginning of the film. This is also when Ripley's ability to drive them is planted. Our attention is distracted by the macho attitude of two of the men who don't believe she can do anything useful (conflict for Ripley). Although the exoskeleton looks cool, it doesn't look like it can be used as a weapon, so we don't guess that it's going to be used in a key scene later. Also, the loader makes it possible to defeat the alien queen, but it doesn't make it easy: Ripley has to fight hard to win that final battle, and she's instrumental in securing the outcome.

One last thing: a *deus ex machina* can also creep in at the end of a dramatic sequence or the climax of a scene, if you use the fractal aspect of story structure and design parts of your screenplay (acts, sequences, scenes, subplots, strands) with a main dramatic action. So look for them everywhere, not only at the ending, and try to avoid them.

That is, unless you decide to make fun of them, as in *Adaptation*, which ends with a *deus ex machina* planted during the hilarious Robert McKee lecture, or *Deadpool 2*, with a character whose main characteristic is to be incredibly lucky (Domino). Again, everything is possible, as long as you know what you're doing – and as long as the audience knows you know what you're doing.

Solutions

So how do we avoid a *deus ex machina* at the end of a story?

✓ **Plant the help** that is going to make it possible for the protagonist to overcome the obstacle **before it is needed**. This help can be an ability (something that the character can do), an object (for example, something that can be used as a weapon), or a character who's able to help.

✓ **Make sure that you distract the audience during the plant**, so that we don't guess that whatever is being planted will be used later to help the protagonist out of a difficult situation. The best way to distract the audience is to use conflict. So use humorous or serious conflict between the characters to establish the element that needs planting without allowing the audience to focus on it. See the *Gravity*, *Adaptation*, and *Aliens* examples above.

✓ **The planted element should only make it *possible* for the protagonist to overcome the situation**. It should never make it *easy*. So despite the planted help, it should still be difficult for the protagonist to succeed.

✓ **The protagonist should be active in the use of the planted element**. It's not enough, for example, to plant the existence of a weapon if someone else uses it, or to plant a potentially helpful character if that character single-handedly resolves the situation. The protagonist should be involved and part of the solution, even if the planted element is ultimately what makes the solution possible.

✓ A *deus ex machina* can also happen at the end of a character-led story, if the character finally manages to change, but we have no idea why. **So make sure that the protagonist's evolution is a consequence of the action,** especially of the conflict experienced by the protagonist. We tend to resist change, it's conflict that forces us to change. This is a key part of designing a satisfying character-led story.

Connected Problems in This Book

- 22 The Ending Is an Anti-Climax
- 26 The Villains or Antagonists Are Weak or Unconvincing
- 10 The Ending Doesn't Work

Sections in Screenwriting Unchained

- 'Planting and Pay-Off' in 2.1 Behind the Scenes, especially 'Avoiding a Deus ex Machina in *Gravity*'
- 'Time-Locks', 'Climax vs Ending' and 'Happy Ending vs Satisfying Ending' in 2.3 Craft the Draft

Sections in 12 Ways to a Stronger Screenplay

- Planting and Pay-Off, Visual Storytelling
- A Satisfying Ending

24 There Is No Clear Antagonist

Although this is a fairly common note, not having an antagonist in a story isn't necessarily a problem, depending on its story-type. Conflict is needed in every story, for many reasons and in many forms, but that conflict doesn't necessarily come from an antagonist. An antagonist is simply the most conventional way to generate conflict.

So let's try to identify what lies behind this note.

First of all, what is an antagonist?

An antagonist isn't the same as a villain. A villain is a conceptually negative character whose goal is perceived as negative: destroying the world, killing people, etc. An antagonist is a character or group of characters whose goal is in direct opposition to the protagonist's goal, and so is the source of most of the conflict in the story. Most villains are antagonists, but not all antagonists have to be villains.

So while you might need a villain in say superhero stories, an antagonist can be a more subtle, more complex character, because they don't need to be conceptually negative or have a negative goal / motivation. For example, Billy's father in *Billy Elliot* is an antagonist – the source of most of the conflict for Billy in the story – because he doesn't want his son to become a ballet dancer, but that's because he's prejudiced, not because he doesn't love his son, or doesn't want what he thinks is the best for him. It's also because he hasn't been able to move on from the death of his wife, and rejects everything connected to her as he's trying not to think about her. None of this makes him a villain. Just someone who suffers, who struggles to move on, and as a result is at risk of damaging his relationship with his son as well as his son's ability to realise his full potential.

In some stories, we have an antagonistic force rather than an antagonist. This is often the case in disaster movies: *Gravity* (space), *Everest* (a mountain), *Twister* (tornadoes) and *The Towering Inferno* (a fire) to name a few. In these stories, the co-protagonists, who share the same goal of surviving, are often sources of conflict too, because they disagree on how to survive, or cause problems because of the way they deal (or fail to deal) with the situation.

It's also possible to have no antagonist because in some stories there is no need for one, or because the protagonist *is* the antagonist. This is usually determined by the story-type.

In **plot-led stories**, we are more likely to have an antagonist and benefit from one, because the main problem in the story lies outside the protagonist, and this problem might have a single source. Whether it's a **single character** (nurse Annie in *Misery*, the shark in *Jaws*, an android in *The Terminator*); a **group of characters sharing the same goal** (the aliens in *Aliens*, the bandits in *The Magnificent Seven*, the agents in *The Matrix)*; or an **antagonistic force** as in disaster movies, usually nature, as mentioned earlier.

But it's also fine to have more than one single source of conflict, coming from antagonistic characters with different goals. This is the case in *Midnight Run*. Here, we have the Mafia with Serrano and his goons, Alonso and the FBI, Marvin and the bounty hunters, and of course The Duke himself. So we have lots of antagonistic characters and no clear antagonist (although we have a villain in Serrano).

In **character-led stories** (where the main problem lies within the protagonist), there is no need for an antagonist because the protagonist *is* the antagonist. The main source of conflict comes from the protagonist fighting an internal flaw, resisting change. So if you get this note, it might be because your protagonist isn't facing enough conflict, or that conflict isn't clear to the audience.

It could also be because the protagonist isn't facing a strong enough dilemma as they struggle between their conscious want and unconscious need, which should be pulling them in opposite directions. For example, in *Silver Linings Playbook*, Pat wants to get back together with his wife, Nikki, but we know that what he needs is to move on so he can end up with Tiffany. Will he fail to change and so go back to Nikki, or will he cease to be deluded and embrace his future with Tiffany? This is the dilemma explored for most of the story until the climax of the film.

Character-led stories show a protagonist fighting against themselves. Antagonistic characters in these are often catalyst characters, i.e. characters that look like antagonists opposing the protagonist's conscious want, but are, in fact, co-protagonists helping them move towards their unconscious need to change. Tiffany in *Silver Linings Playbook* is such a catalyst character for Pat, as is The Duke for Jack Walsh in *Midnight Run*. Making this distinction between an antagonist and a catalyst is key to understanding how character-led stories are designed, and why they are different from plot-led stories. An *antagonist* in a plot-led story *opposes* the protagonist. A *catalyst* in a character-led story – or the character-led subplot of a plot-led story – *helps* the protagonist to change. Both relationships look conflictual, but they are fundamentally different.

In **theme-led stories** (multi-stranded narratives where the main problem usually lies in society), there is no main antagonist as there is no main protagonist, given that there is no main plot, only subplots called strands. There is, usually, a protagonist in each strand. There can be an antagonist in some of the strands if they are plot-led, but it's not an obligation. The real antagonist tends to be society, because that's where the main problem usually lies in theme-led stories: *Crash*, *Magnolia* and *Traffic* among them.

Sometimes, the protagonist in one strand can be an antagonist in some or all the others, as in *Game of Thrones*. What's important here is to be aware of how conflict is managed and how identification is made possible with one or more characters in the story.

Solutions

To sum it up, if you want to deal with this note:

✓   **Identify the story-type of your project** (plot-led, character-led, theme-led or hybrid / exception).

✓   **Check whether having no clear antagonist in your story is a problem.** In a **plot-led story**, you might need a clear antagonist, but if your protagonist is set against various sources of conflict, it's not necessarily a problem. In a

character-led story, the protagonist *is* the antagonist and you might need a catalyst character instead. In a **theme-led story,** there is usually no main antagonist, though society is often the main source of conflict.

✓ Remember that **if this note comes up, it usually means that there isn't enough conflict in the story for the protagonist,** or that the reader can't understand it or relate to it. So while the note itself might be misguided – because not having a clear antagonist isn't necessarily a problem – you have to go beyond it and assess whether there's still a problem that needs fixing.

If there is a lack of conflict for the protagonist, or if the reader can't understand or relate to this conflict, or if nothing can be done about it, or if no one cares about the conflict because there's nothing at stake, then address this in the next draft – using the sections linked below – even if there is no need for a clear antagonist in the story. This should resolve the issue. That's the magic of addressing the problem instead of focusing on the symptom.

Connected Problems in This Book

- 26 The Villains or Antagonists Are Weak or Unconvincing
- 18 There Is No Clear Protagonist
- 01 We Don't Care About the Protagonist
- 20 The Conflict Is Artificial or Inconsequential

Sections in Screenwriting Unchained

- 'Managing Conflict' and 'Managing Information' in 2.1 Behind the Scenes
- 'Hero vs Protagonist', 'Protagonist vs Antagonist' and 'Villain vs Antagonist' in 2.3 Craft the Draft
- 3.3 Grow the draft
- 4.3 Weave the Draft

Sections in 12 Ways to a Stronger Screenplay

- Managing Conflict (Who Wants / Needs What and Why?)

- Managing Information (Who Knows What When?)
- Antagonist or Catalyst: Who Is Pushing Your Protagonist?

25 The Narrative Is Episodic or Repetitive

Episodic means that the story feels like a succession of short stories that are unconnected to each other. The aim should be to create a unified story, where scenes build on each other and the value of the whole story is more than its parts.

Repetitive means that the same or similar action repeats itself in a predictable and often boring fashion. For example, the way the protagonist tries to reach a goal leads to a repetition of similar scenes or sequences, without enough progression. Or there is little variation in how the protagonist tries to change or faces a dilemma over the course of the story.

These two symptoms are connected because they find their root in the same problem: a lack of *causality* (cause and effect) in the story.

This happens when it's possible to swap scenes or sequences, or even take some out of the story entirely, without impacting on the story negatively or making it harder to understand.

The objective should be for each scene to have consequences in later scenes or sequences, and as storytellers, we should make sure events in a scene or a sequence stem from what has happened previously. This brings causality to a story.

Even if a situation repeats itself, new elements or variations should be brought into each scene and sequence, so that it feels fresh. Changing the location, the props or the characters isn't enough to avoid a feeling of repetition. The nature of the dramatic action itself has to be different; it has to take into account what happened before and impact on what happens next.

This is closely related to foreshadowing, which means planting an element that pays off later. The more planting and pay-off in a story, the more causality. It's also connected to managing information, especially dramatic irony and surprise. For example, the same situation can repeat itself, but if we know something that at least some of the characters don't, it can create a very satisfying effect. Films like *Groundhog Day, Source Code* and *The Edge of Tomorrow* (*Live. Die. Repeat.*) are entirely based on this combination of planting, pay-off and dramatic irony. Each repetition pays off of a previous cycle, and it usually involves dramatic irony: we know something that one or more characters don't know. The sequence in *Groundhog Day* where Phil tries to use his knowledge of Rita's taste and aspirations to seduce her is a great illustration of this.

In these examples, the repetitive element is part of the high-concept at the core of the story and the use of planting and dramatic irony means that they never feel repetitive or episodic.

Solutions

So how do we address this note?

- ✓ **Check for causality.** Write a step outline (the whole story over a few pages with one paragraph per key step) and see if you can take out or swap some of these steps without disrupting the whole story. If this is possible, then either get rid of these steps or find a way to connect them with what has happened previously and what happens next. Pay extra attention to subplots and verify that they are connected to the main plot.

- ✓ **Raise the stakes.** Make sure that obstacles, conflict, antagonists, dilemmas grow in strength and intensity and that things get more challenging as the story unfolds.

- ✓ **Look at the way you manage conflict in the story.** In a **plot-led story** (where the main problem lies outside the protagonist), break down the main action into dramatic sequences, making sure all are connected to the same conscious goal and all progress in intensity. In a **character-led story** (where the main problem lies within the protagonist), break down the main evolution and check that the main psychological or emotional steps mapping the protagonist's change happen in the right order and are clearly caused by the conflict that the characters experience. You can also do this for the character-led subplot in a plot-led story. In a **theme-led story** (multi-stranded narrative where the main problem usually lies in society), check that most of your strands are structured as either plot-led or character-led subplots, and that each strand is connected to the same theme.

✓   **Look at the way you manage information in the story.** Think about twists and surprises (properly seeded before) that could break any feeling of predictability within the main dramatic action or evolution. How can you upset expectations? Can you reveal a piece of information that brings in a new obstacle, leads to a change of plan, sets-up a dramatic irony, etc? As mentioned earlier, *Groundhog Day, Edge of Tomorrow* or *Source Code* are repetitive by design but they use foreshadowing and dramatic irony to turn this episodic aspect of the design into a high-concept story.

✓   **Think of a possible time-lock to increase tension.** Action thrillers are not the only stories that can benefit from a time-lock (a limited time to achieve a goal or subgoal). If your story has to be repetitive, increasing tension with a time-lock can make this aspect of the narrative more bearable. For example, in *Two Days, One Night* protagonist Sandra wants to get her job back. The story could feel repetitive as she tries to convince each of her colleagues to vote for her keeping her job rather than them getting a bonus, but the time-lock increases the tension by giving her just two days and one night to reach her goal.

Connected Problems in This Book

- 07 The Story Sags in the Middle
- 29 The Plot Is Slowed Down By Unconnected Storylines
- 16 The Scenes Are Aimless, There Is No Dramatic Conflict
- 17 The Script Loses the Plot in the Third Act
- 22 The Ending Is an Anti-Climax
- 04 The Story Is Linear, Feels Predictable

Sections in Screenwriting Unchained

- 2.2 Sequence the Action and 2.3 Craft the Draft
- 3.2 Sequence the Evolution and 3.3 Grow the Draft
- 4.2 Sequence the Strands and 4.3 Weave the Draft

Sections in 12 Ways to a Stronger Screenplay

- Fractal Aspect of Story Structure
- Managing Conflict
- Managing Information
- Time-Lock
- Planting, Pay-Off and Visual Storytelling

26 The Villains or Antagonists Are Weak or Unconvincing

First off, we don't need an antagonist and even less a villain in every story, as explained in 24 There Is No Clear Antagonist. But when we do, they have to be convincing. Their originality and strength can make or break a story.

What can make antagonists weak and unconvincing?

1) **Sometimes antagonists are weak because writers unconsciously protect the protagonist.** Although this is understandable, putting our protagonist in a protective bubble will harm the story. Or it could be that we are focusing on the protagonist (who is often a version of ourselves, so a character we feel close to), and we're not looking at the story from the point of view of their nemesis. This is a fundamental mistake. As writers, we should channel Don Corleone in *The Godfather*: "Keep your friends close – and your enemies closer". This doesn't mean that the audience has to approve of the antagonist, condone their actions or even like the character, but we need to know the antagonist just as well as the protagonist. We should understand their goal, motivation and their decisions so that they make sense. Putting ourselves in the antagonist's shoes should help us to come up with stronger obstacles for the protagonist, hence make the antagonist more convincing.

2) **Antagonists can be weak and unconvincing if they are bland characters.** This rarely works. In successful protagonist-antagonist stories, the antagonist is often more fascinating and interesting than the protagonist, especially in thrillers, horror movies or monster stories. We should identify emotionally with the protagonist, fear

for them and experience the story from their point of view, but we should be fascinated by the antagonist, their evolution or the evolution of our perception of them. Think about films like *Jaws, Misery, Alien, The Dark Knight*: emotionally, we are with the protagonist, yet we are captivated by the antagonist (a shark, crazy Nurse Annie, an alien, the Joker). The antagonists in these films are often more fascinating than the protagonists even if emotionally, we're rooting for Chief Brody and his two co-protagonists, for writer Paul Sheldon, for Ripley and the crew of the Nostromo or for Bruce Wayne / Batman and Commissioner Gordon.

3) Often, antagonists are weak because they are too simplistic. Two-dimensional, moustache-twirling villains don't cut it anymore in modern storytelling, even for children. For more on this, you might want to look at the difference between an antagonist and a villain, explained in <u>24 There Is No Clear Antagonist</u>. Understanding this is key to creating more complex antagonists. An antagonist can be a conceptually nice character, someone who wants the best for the protagonist, someone who genuinely loves the protagonist, but needs to change their own values. For example, in *Billy Elliot*, Billy's father evolves from antagonist to co-protagonist, once he accepts that Billy should be true to himself. He isn't an abusive father to Billy, he simply needs to move on from the death of his wife and not be afraid of Billy being so like his mother in order to overcome his prejudice. The problem, for Billy's father, isn't that Billy is dancing, it's that the dancing is reminding him of his grief, which he is trying to suppress. So you can absolutely think about the evolution of your antagonist, and map it as you would map the evolution of a protagonist.

Overall, the sooner you forget the notion of villain (a negative character who opposes the hero) and embrace the concept of antagonist (a character or group of characters whose goal is in direct opposition to the protagonist), the sooner you'll design strong and convincing antagonists.

So look at the story from the point of view of the antagonist, come up with a clear goal and motivation and simply make sure that the antagonist doesn't experience more conflict than the protagonist, or if they do momentarily that this causes even more conflict for the protagonist later on.

Once you master this, you can blur the lines further, but this requires a very specific talent.

For example, in *Heat*, there isn't really a clear protagonist or antagonist, yet it doesn't prevent the film from working. You can identify with bank robber Neil McCauley, or with detective Vincent Hanna. You can even identify with both. Identifying means "feeling empathy", "understanding". It doesn't mean liking or approving of. For me, McCauley is the protagonist overall, but that's subjective. It might simply be because his conflict resonates more with me than Hanna's conflict. Ultimately, it doesn't really matter as long as everyone can identify emotionally with at least one character in the story.

Solutions

To sum it up, here are a few tips to address this note:

✓ **Don't protect your protagonist.** This will make your antagonist weaker. A good antagonist should be the main source of conflict for the protagonist, so they have to be clever and resourceful in order to be worthy opponents.

✓ **Don't settle for a bland or simplistic antagonist.** Make them original. Find a character trait or motivation we've never seen before. The stories we tell are often similar. What makes them stand out are the characters. If you have an antagonist in a story, dedicate as much time – if not more – to their design and avoid clichés.

✓ **Remember that antagonists can evolve too.** Billy's father in *Billy Elliot*, the Stasi officer in *The Lives of Others* – these characters start as antagonistic figures and gradually become co-protagonists or even protagonists. So it can be useful to map the evolution of an antagonist as you would for a protagonist. Just make sure that the evolution, if any, is caused by the conflict and the events experienced in the story.

✓ **Think about the antagonist as the protagonist of their own story.** For example, the Joker in *The Dark Knight* doesn't see himself as a villain. He has an objective and a motivation. He is an agent of chaos. He isn't motivated by money, he's seeking anarchy. You could certainly argue that the Joker is a large part of the success of *The Dark Knight*, and not only because of Heath Ledger's extraordinary performance. The Joker is a well fleshed-out, three-dimensional antagonist: intriguing, complex but readable, unpredictable yet fully coherent.

✓ **Going through the story from the antagonist's point of view** can be an interesting exercise, and can help clarify the motivation and evolution of the character. It can also be done literally: some stories are told from the point of view of the antagonist, whether the antagonist remains so (*The Hand That Rocks the Cradle*) or becomes a co-protagonist (*The Lives of Others*).

✓ **If you're working on an adaptation, you could even consider making the antagonist of the original material (fairy tale, novel, real event) the protagonist of the story.** This is what Linda Wolverton does brilliantly in *Maleficent*, offering a subversive vision of the familiar Perrault tale. How do we turn an antagonist into a protagonist? By focusing most of the conflict on them. The protagonist is the character who experiences the most conflict in the story. Classically, it's a conceptually nice character (hero or heroine), but the story can become more complex, original and interesting if you structure it over a character that isn't conceptually nice, yet experiences the most conflict. If you do that, remember that you need a strong antagonist for your antagonist-turned-protagonist, unless of course you make it a character-led story, which is what *Maleficent* is. This can work in biopics too, for example in *Amadeus*, where the protagonist is Salieri while Mozart is the main character.

Connected Problems in This Book

Sections in Screenwriting Unchained

- 'Protagonist vs Antagonist' and 'Villain vs Antagonist' in 2.3 Craft the Draft
- 3.3 Grow the Draft
- 4.3 Weave the Draft

Sections in 12 Ways to a Stronger Screenplay

- Antagonist or Catalyst: Who Is Testing Your Protagonist?

27 The Script Is Cold, Unemotional

There can be all sorts of reasons for this note. Let's look at a few of them.

First, it could be the writer's intention to write a cold, unemotional script. Often, this is because the writer wants to make an intellectual point, or wants the audience to think while they experience the story, and they feel that strong emotions would get in the way. There is nothing wrong being a didactic writer, but it has consequences.

The key to developing a cold, unemotional story is to be aware of its limited potential audience and so be realistic about budget and potential financing partners. As long as this is kept in mind, this note can be ignored, provided it doesn't come from a key source of finance. Cold, unemotional stories can find an audience, it just tends to be a small one.

Most people expect a story to deliver a combination of meaning, entertainment and emotion. A masterpiece is a story that delivers all these elements in one complete package, though not necessarily at the same time. Ideally, entertainment and emotion during the story, food for thought afterwards. If we think during the storytelling process, it should be about story elements (trying to solve a mystery for example), not about philosophical considerations. That comes later. A good story usually delivers both an emotional and an intellectual gratification, but getting this balance right is essential.

Occasionally a writer might want to impress with their erudition. If that's you, try to let go. This isn't what a good story is about. Drama is about putting strong, original characters into situations that reveal a universal side of the human psyche. If that's done with talent, a writer will certainly look clever, but so much more so if it wasn't their main objective.

Solutions

Assuming that writing a cold, unemotional piece isn't the writer's intention, how do we address this?

- ✓ **First, look inward**. Are you cold and unemotional? Are you repressing your own emotions? I won't make an attempt at cheap therapy here, that's too complex a subject. Still, some writers repress their own emotions yet excel at writing emotional pieces. Others struggle with characters' emotions because they repress their own. If either of these examples describes you, find a way to deal with it as it's going to be difficult otherwise to address this issue.

- ✓ **Without being emotionally repressed, some writers are not ready or willing to reveal enough of themselves**. This is often a form of self-protection, especially when we're too close to the problem (say writing about a break up after we've just experienced one). We sometimes need some distance to be able to write about an issue close to our heart, even if our personal life often fuels the fiction that we write. "Write what you know" means writing about emotions you understand, so don't be afraid to pull from your personal emotional experience, even if writing a genre film. Just make sure that your feelings are not too raw. Writing can be therapeutic, but its primary aim shouldn't be to offer the writer therapy. If you're too close to a subject, find a less direct way to explore it, or put it on the back burner and get back to it when you're ready.

- ✓ **Other times, we might find it difficult to write honestly about something because we're afraid of being judged**. Not only by the audience, but also by our peers, our friends, our family: *What will they think if I write honestly about this situation, about these characters, about these feelings?* As a consequence, you're not allowing your characters to reveal a key part of yourself, a part that should be revealed in the story you're writing. You're trying not to upset a partner or a parent who might read your script or watch your film. You're anticipating how your peers will react to your work. You have to put this fear aside. Don't worry about what people *who know you* will think of you when they read your story / watch your film. Instead, focus on what people *who don't know you* will experience when they enter the world of your characters and share their journey.

✓ **Another tough question: do you care about your characters?** Do you understand them? Do you know them? Is what happens in the story dictated by who the characters are and the decisions they make, or by what you want to happen in the story? How can your audience care about your characters and understand them if you don't? This isn't only true for the protagonist, but also for the other characters, including the antagonist when there is one.

✓ **An easier question, but no less important: what's at stake?** Sometimes the story feels cold because there is no tension, no pressure, no heat. Raise the stakes, put your characters in a situation that forces them to get out of their comfort zone, that forces them to reveal who they truly are, or that leads them to change and evolve. This is hard to achieve in an everyday situation. I'm not saying that characters should be abducted by aliens, just that the story should explore an extreme situation for that character. For example, leaving the institution where he feels secure is an extreme situation for Raymond Babbit in *Rain Man*.

✓ **A mysterious backstory could make it impossible for the audience to identify emotionally with your protagonist**, and so make the story feel cold and unemotional. You might want to look at 30 The Script Contains Too Much Exposition, especially the part where *Cake* is discussed. Claire Bennett isn't cold or unemotional, but the story feels cold for a long time because she knows key things about her past that she doesn't share with us. If that sounds like your story, you might want to look at getting the right balance of exposition in the story: not too much, but just enough, at the right time.

✓　**Move from the intellectual sphere to the emotional sphere**. This doesn't mean having stupid characters in stupid stories, or depriving the audience of intellectual gratification. It means creating drama. Showing a human action or evolution (or more than one in a theme-led story) that leads the audience to identify with at least one character. To achieve this, you have to **manage conflict and information**. You need to design a dramatic situation that will throw your characters against each other and reveal who they really are. Which means that some of *you*, the part of *you* that's in your character, has to be revealed too.

Connected Problems in This Book

- 19 The Script Feels Formulaic
- 01 We Don't Care About the Protagonist
- 02 We Don't Care About the Story
- 05 The Characters Are Flat, Two-Dimensional
- 16 The Scenes Are Aimless, There Is No Dramatic Conflict
- 21 There Is Too Much Dialogue
- 30 The Script Contains Too Much Exposition

Sections in Screenwriting Unchained

- 'Managing Conflict' and 'Managing Information' in 2.1 Behind the Scenes
- 'Happy Ending vs. Satisfying Ending' in 2.3 Craft the Draft

Sections in 12 Ways to a Stronger Screenplay

- Story-Type and Genre
- Managing Conflict (Who Wants/Needs what and Why?)
- Managing Information (Who Knows What When?)
- Satisfying Ending

28 The Protagonist Is Not Strong Enough

The usual ways of addressing this note are debatable, mainly because there is a great deal of confusion around the notion of a protagonist. Sometimes, our protagonist should indeed be stronger, but this comment often points to a symptom rather than to the actual problem.

First, let's define what a protagonist is

1) **The character who experiences the most conflict in the story**, hence the character with whom we identify the most at an emotional level. It comes from the Greek word *protagonistes*, which means "the one who fights in the first row". This definition applies to many stories, but not all, as discussed in 18 There Is No Clear Protagonist.

2) **A character we can relate to at an emotional level.** We don't have to like the character, or approve of their actions. We simply have to know enough about them so that they come across as real human beings, and we have to understand the conflict they face. If their conflict is universal, it will be possible for a wide range of people to relate to them. The less universal the conflict, the more difficult it becomes to relate to the character, which restricts the potential audience. This is where Maslow's Hierarchy of Needs can help: some human needs (survival, protection of loved ones, safety) are shared by almost every single human being on the planet; others (self-actualisation, for example) aren't. Taking this into consideration can help when it comes to choosing the right protagonist in each story and can increase your chances of reaching a wider audience, if this is your goal. Picking the right kind of conflict is also crucial in terms of raising the stakes, which can be

key to increasing the audience's interest in the protagonist. See <u>01</u> <u>We Don't Care About the Protagonist</u>.

3) A character we understand and care about. This means understanding the conflict they face, as explained above. But it also means understanding their decisions.

In **plot-led stories** (where the main problem lies outside the protagonist), as soon as a character does something stupid (unless that's part of the character's personality, say, in a comedy), we lose our connection to them, because we no longer feel that they are like us – even if we've identified with them during the whole film. If, for example, at the end of a thriller, the protagonist decides for no good reason to venture alone into a dark, scary place where we know – and they know – a serial killer is waiting for them, we will most probably lose faith in them and won't care whether they get killed or not. Why not call the police? Should they get killed, their stupidity makes us feel that they deserved it. And if they survive, we get no relief or satisfaction because we've stopped caring. This is brilliantly avoided in the climax of *The Silence of the Lambs*: We realise that Clarice is stepping into the killer's den the minute he opens the door, but she doesn't know because unlike us, she's never seen him before. The audience thinks the killer is being arrested by her colleagues miles away, so we're shocked when we understand that's not the case, and the tension before she realises the situation in unbearable... This is a great example of generating suspense with dramatic irony (we are aware of the danger, she isn't), while keeping the protagonist strong and clever. Had Clarice known that the killer might be in this isolated house and had gone there on her own without having a good reason to do so, it would have weakened her as a character and our emotional involvement during the climax would have been significantly reduced.

In **character-led stories**, when the character is struggling with an internal flaw, they often make the wrong decisions, yet we feel their pain because we understand, before they do, their need to change. We can understand them and care about them despite them making the wrong decisions because we understand their internal problem, and how it leads them to make these mistakes. For example, in *Silver Linings Playbook*, Pat is deluded. He thinks he has his bipolarity under control and he wants the wrong thing: to get back together with his wife, Nikki. We know better: He needs to move on, to get better, to end up with Tiffany. Another example of dramatic irony, even if it's a more diffuse one.

4) A character we can invest our hope in. This is absolutely key in creating a protagonist the audience will be willing to invest in emotionally. We need to be able to believe that the protagonist could potentially reach their goal (in **plot-led stories**) or be able to change (in **character-led stories**). This hope for the character to succeed should be matched by a fear that they might fail. We have to constantly strike the right balance between hope and fear. This is because as soon as we understand who wants or needs what and why in a story, we get drawn into the dramatic question: Will the protagonist succeed or fail? This is a very powerful hook; in fact it's the main hook that leads the audience to want to know what's going to happen next. If it looks like it's going to be too easy, because the protagonist seems too strong given the obstacles they face, then we're able to answer this question too early. And if it feels too difficult, if it looks like the protagonist doesn't stand a chance of succeeding, then we're not interested either: Nobody wants to be a loser. If it looks like the protagonist is bound to fail, who will want to identify with, to *become*, that character? In that case, you might need to make it clearer how it's going to be difficult *but possible* for the protagonist to reach their conscious goal or to change.

5) A character who comes across as entirely original. You want us to feel that we've never seen this character before. Even if you have to find some universality in your protagonist, so that we can relate to their conflict and aspirations, you also have to find a way to make this character unique. Find universality in the backbone, the aspirations, the goal and the need. Create an archetype with a clear main characteristic. Then find uniqueness in the details. Salieri in *Amadeus* is jealous, like Othello. Same archetype, yet they are very different characters. Salieri's love of food and relationship to God make him a unique "jealous character" in the repertoire.

Now, let's clarify what a protagonist does not have to be

1) The main character. The main character is the title character, the character whose life is the subject of the story, possibly the most well-known character or the character with the most screen time.

This is not necessarily the protagonist. For example, *Amadeus* is about Mozart's life but the protagonist is Salieri. In many horror films, the main character, the most interesting character, is the antagonist, the monster. We identify emotionally with the protagonist, but are fascinated by the antagonist.

2) The point-of-view character. Although it's unusual, some stories are told using primarily the point of view of a character who isn't the protagonist. For example, *The Lives of Others* or *The Hand That Rocks the Cradle* both start with the point of view of the antagonist. In the second example, Peyton remains the antagonist until the end. In the first example, Stasi officer Wiesler is the antagonist, point-of-view character and main character to start with, but he gradually becomes a co-protagonist, while remaining the main character. This is because in the first half of the film, the couple he is spying on experience more conflict than he does: they are victims of a strong dramatic irony (they don't know he's spying on them), so are not aware of the danger, which is an efficient way to generate tension and suspense. This is what makes us identify with them rather than him, and see them as protagonists even if they are not very active. This shows how the notion of protagonist, antagonist and main character are closely linked, but also how managing conflict and managing information are key factors in leading the audience to identifying with one character rather than another.

3) The character who changes most in the story. This is a misconception brought about in the last few decades that has caused much confusion and led to many clichés. In **plot-led stories**, there is no need for the character to change because the main problem lies outside the protagonist. The protagonist can evolve (they learn, they grow), but they rarely need to change because there is nothing fundamentally wrong with them (or the story would be character-led). In **character-led stories**, it's the opposite: the main problem lies within the protagonist, so they *do* need to change. While having some form of evolution in a story is a good idea, it's not the degree of change that determines who the protagonist is. It's which character experiences the most conflict. **In both character-led and plot-led stories**, the protagonist experiences the most conflict, struggling with external foes or internal woes.

For example, in classic action / adventure movies (*Indiana Jones, James Bond, John Wick, Mission Impossible*), the characters don't change. That's because there is nothing essentially wrong with them. The same goes for many sitcoms and comedies (*Friends, The Big Bang Theory*). Most of the characters are flawed, and that's why they make us laugh. In real life, they would need to change, but in fiction we don't want them to because if they did, they wouldn't be funny anymore. So forget this metric as a way of deciding who your protagonist is, and concentrate on the amount of conflict experienced by each character. This is usually a much more useful indicator.

4) A conceptually nice character. Another truly damaging "solution" when it's hard to identify with a protagonist: Let's make the character nicer! This is not only irrelevant, it can be very damaging, especially if the whole point of the story is to have a negative character who needs to change. Phil Connors and Melvin Udall are not nice characters at the beginning of *Groundhog Day* or *As Good as it Gets.* That's exactly how they are meant to be. Making them nicer would go against the story itself. The real involvement for an audience comes from wanting that character to change, to become a better person. This can be achieved through a redeeming character trait (for example, Phil Connors is not only self-centred and arrogant, he is also funny). A charismatic actor can also bring a degree of humanity to an unsympathetic protagonist. This might help to draw the audience closer to the character and get them involved in wanting the character to change.

5) Someone like us (same language, same culture, same country of origin, same interests). We've already defined the elements that make a strong protagonist: a character who experiences the most conflict, a character we can relate to because we understand their conflict. We can identify with a robot who falls in love (*Wall-E*), an alien who wants to go home (*E.T.*), a toy jealous of another toy (*Toy Story*), a Mayan hunter who protects his family (*Apocalypto*) or a disfigured man who seeks acceptance as a human being (*The Elephant Man*) because they face conflicts that most humans can relate to. They may be very different from us, some of them are not even human, yet it doesn't prevent us from identifying with them. Protagonists don't have to be the same age as their target audience, speak the same language or be of the same sex, as long as we can relate to their goals, aspirations and emotions. If we're human – let's exclude sociopaths – we can feel empathy towards anyone who experiences human emotions and conflict that we can relate to. This is the beauty of drama: it works better if it focuses on what is common to all human beings than if it tries to capitalise on superficial differences to segment an audience. Let the distributor worry about this: it's rarely a useful storytelling element.

6) An active protagonist. Drama means action, so it's easier to deal with an active protagonist, but this doesn't mean that a passive or reactive protagonist can't be just as efficient, depending on the story-type or the genre. We want the audience to feel that someone is doing something about the main problem, but it doesn't have to be done consciously. **Plot-led stories** are designed around a main dramatic action, so the protagonist has to be active at some point. Often in thrillers they are reactive rather than active: It's usually the antagonist who sets the story in motion in thrillers, not the protagonist. In **character-led stories**, it's a main evolution that shapes the story, so a passive or reactive protagonist is much less of an issue, as long as their internal problem has been clearly defined and the audience understands what's really at stake. It isn't what the protagonist *wants*, but what the protagonist *needs*.

7) A single individual. A protagonist can indeed be a group of people sharing the same dramatic goal in a **plot-led story**, such as the crew of the Nostromo led by Ripley in *Alien*, the soldiers led by Captain John Miller in *Saving Private Ryan* or the group of survivors in *Bird Box*. Although rare, it can also be a group of characters sharing the same need in a **character-led story**. For example, the whole family in *Little Miss Sunshine*, whose members have the common conscious goal of getting Olive to the pageant, while their common unconscious need is to become less dysfunctional. In **theme-led stories** (multi-stranded narratives) or **hybrids and exceptions**, often there is no main protagonist, or we have a succession of protagonists, so the story works differently.

Solutions

Understanding more clearly what a protagonist is – and what it doesn't have to be – hopefully has helped you to decide whether this note was deserved or not. For example, if you're developing a plot-led story and if your protagonist is so weak that we can't see how they could possibly succeed, then you might want to retune the balance between the strength of the protagonist and the strength of the obstacles, making it easier to invest emotionally in their journey. However, in some cases, this weakness might be the internal obstacle at the core of a character-led story, in which case it would not make sense to make them stronger from the get go. They might need to get stronger, but that's precisely their journey. They should, however, be resilient and not give up easily despite their weaknesses.

Overall, what the note most likely means is that you either have a weak protagonist who needs to become stronger or more active, or you haven't made it clear enough to the audience that what was really at stake wasn't what the character wanted but what the character needed.

If your story fits the latter, Maslow's Hierarchy of Needs might help, because it's difficult for a character to focus – even unconsciously – on their need to change when their life is in danger, unless the need to change is what's going to make their survival possible.

This is usually about clarity in the story design. In a thriller for example, the character's need to grow (say Ryan Stone's need to move on from her daughter's death in *Gravity*) will be related to a problem sitting higher on Maslow's Hierarchy of Needs than the main problem, which is to survive.

So if you're developing a character-led story and if you want the main problem to be about love / belonging, self-esteem or self-actualisation, make sure that you don't put the protagonist's life in danger (hence raise a problem about survival or safety), or the audience might struggle to understand why they don't drop their existential issues to concentrate on surviving, as most of us would.

For more on this, please see Is Maslow Running the Show? in the first chapter of *Screenwriting Unchained*.

Connected Problems in This Book

*   01 We Don't Care About the Protagonist
*   18 There Is No Clear Protagonist
*   24 There Is No Clear Antagonist

Emmanuel Oberg

- 26 The Villains or Antagonists Are Weak or Unconvincing
- 13 The Characters Are Stereotypes or Clichés

Sections in Screenwriting Unchained

- 1.3 Is Maslow Running the Show?
- Choosing the Best Protagonist on 2.2 Sequence the Action
- 'Managing Conflict', 'Protagonist vs Antagonist' and 'Hero vs Protagonist' in 2.3 Craft the Draft
- 3.3 Grow the Draft
- 3.4 Hands-On: Growth, Change or Steadfast?

Sections in 12 Ways to a Stronger Screenplay

- Antagonist or Catalyst: Who Is Testing Your Protagonist?

29 The Plot Is Slowed Down By Unconnected Storylines

Whatever the structure of your script, you are getting this note because too many scenes or subplots seem unconnected to the main part of the story, so the solution tends to be the same: to cut what's not needed or to strengthen the apparent connection with more causality (cause and effect), which usually involves more planting and pay-off.

As a first step, you might want to read 25 The Narrative Is Episodic or Repetitive. It explains what a lack of causality means and how to address this at a structural level (for example, without using solely symbolic connections, or through locations or characters, as this is rarely enough).

Now let's look more closely at the main reasons behind this note, taking into account your story-type.

1) You're developing a plot-led story (where the main problem lies outside the protagonist) **or a character-led story** (where the main problem lies within the protagonist), and you're overly focused on storylines that are not sufficiently connected to the main plot.

In such stories, the main plot should be structured either around the main dramatic action (plot-led story) or the main dramatic evolution (character-led story). In other words, the part of the story that's focused on your protagonist's attempts to resolve the main problem, whether it's external or internal.

Subplots are less important dramatic actions or evolutions that often explore a thematic aspect of the story to give it more depth, like Jack Walsh's need to move on from the separation with his wife in *Midnight Run*. The protagonist of these storylines isn't necessarily the protagonist of the film. For example, Sheriff Buster, who attempts to find out what happened to writer Paul Sheldon in

Misery, or Pat's father, who has a gambling addiction in *Silver Linings Playbook*.

These subplots, even if they explore problems that are less important than the main problem in the story, should be connected in some way with the main plot, otherwise you're likely to get the note that "the plot is slowed down by unconnected storylines". If you can take a subplot out and if it doesn't change anything in the story, consider getting rid of it. If it's important to you from a thematic point of view, or because its connection to the main plot becomes more apparent towards the end, find a way to make its connection to the main plot stronger or try to help the audience understand the connection earlier.

2) Or it could be that you're developing a theme-led story (a multi-stranded narrative where the main problem usually lies in society), but the main theme isn't clear, or you have too many themes in the story. In that case, you still have the same problem, which is unconnected storylines, but the solution is different because you don't have a main plot, you have only subplots called strands. Here you have two ways out.

a) Keep developing the story as a multi-stranded narrative in which each strand explores the same theme, but through different characters. Make sure this main theme is clear, so that we understand which common problem the characters are facing in the separate strands. Usually, it's a problem in society or it's a spiritual or philosophical problem, which cannot be solved during the film: racial tension in L.A. (*Crash*), how drugs threaten our society (*Traffic*), how difficult is to be a child, a parent or a grandparent (*Parenthood*), etc. A TV series is also often structured as a theme-led story. For example, the main theme in *Game of Thrones* revolves around power and survival.

b) If, looking at your story, you find that you could structure it around a single main dramatic action or evolution, then consider developing it as either plot-led or character-led. This would mean cutting down the number of subplots to a maximum of two to three, and making sure they are connected to the main plot in some way. More on this in the *Screenwriting Unchained* sections listed at the end of this chapter.

3) If you're developing a hybrid or an exception, then try to look at the way you're managing information, especially if there is a strong dramatic irony (the audience knows something that at least one character is unaware of). It might be that this structural dramatic irony forms the backbone of your story, but you haven't yet found a way to connect it to the other storylines.

Solutions

Beyond the solutions already suggested above, another way to address this issue is to ask yourself: What is the main hook that keeps the attention of the audience over most of the film? If it's the **theme** (what the story is about), you need to make sure that even if you have many storylines they are all connected and explore an interesting theme that is made clear early in the story. Is it an **external problem** that a protagonist is trying to solve consciously, even if some less important internal problems can make this harder? Or is it an **internal problem** related to an unconscious need, even if the protagonist has one or more clear conscious goals in the story? This will help you clarify your story-type, and then decide on the best way to tackle the note.

Connected Problems in This Book

- 25 The Narrative Is Episodic or Repetitive
- 35 The Script Is Unnecessarily Complex
- 20 The Conflict Is Artificial or Inconsequential
- 16 The Scenes Are Aimless, There Is No Dramatic Conflict

Sections in Screenwriting Unchained

- 1.1 What's Wrong with the Three-Act Structure?
- 'Planting and Pay-Off' in 2.1 Behind the Scenes
- 'Don't Forget the Subplots' in 2.2 Sequence the Action
- 3.0 Developing a Character-Led Story
- 4.0 Developing a Theme-Led Story

Sections in 12 Ways to a Stronger Screenplay

- Story-Type and Genre
- Theme (What Is the Story About?)
- Fractal Aspect of Story Structure

- Managing Conflict (Who Wants / Needs What and Why?)
- Managing Information (Who Knows What When?)
- Character (Growth, Change or Steadfast?)
- Planting, Pay-Off and Visual Storytelling

30 The Script Contains Too Much Exposition

Let's define what exposition is, then we'll see why it's a good thing to limit the amount of exposition in a story, and how we can make whatever remains as palatable as possible.

Exposition can have two meanings in screenwriting, so let's first rule out what we're *not* discussing here. Exposition in the context of this note isn't the beginning of a story, the amount of time writers take to set up the characters and the situation before the main dramatic action starts. This used to be called exposition in the old days, but that's not the modern meaning of the word. We call this the set-up instead.

Today, exposition is when we use narration to describe events that happened before the beginning of the story, or sometimes events that happened off screen, between two scenes. The reason why we try to avoid this as much as possible is because it's the literary part of drama. It usually involves someone telling a story about past events (more rarely present or future events), or reading a letter. It's often boring because we want to be shown a story rather than watch characters telling stories to each other.

When exposition is kept to a minimum, for example there is one scene where we briefly learn something about the characters' past, it's usually not an issue. But things get problematic when there is too much exposition. And that's when you get this note.

The key to managing exposition is to find the right balance between what the audience needs to know and what should be kept as backstory.

Although we'll usually try to limit exposition in a story, sometimes we do need to know some key information about the protagonist, what happened to them in the past, so that we can understand who they are, what they want and what they need in the present. We can't identify with the protagonist if they are hiding things from us. We can know more than they do, as in *The Apartment* or *Titanic*, but we shouldn't know less than they do over a long period of time, unless this is the way the whole film is designed, as in *The Usual Suspects*. But in this case, we aren't aware that the main protagonist, Verbal Kint, is hiding something from us. We only discover the manipulation at the end.

What we want to avoid is a situation such as in *Cake*, where Claire Bennett is in a lot of pain, both physically and psychologically, but we have no idea why. To be in that situation for almost half of the film feels alienating to many. We are only able to understand her, her situation and her conflict when we realise what happened to her, and this comes very late in the film. In the first half, she is a stranger. We see her suffer, we feel sorry for her, but we can't identify with her because we're in the dark about a key part of her backstory.

By contrast, in *Silver Linings Playbook*, we learn very quickly everything we need to know to be able to identify with Pat. This is important because we need to be able to decide whether he is right or not to want to get back together with his wife Nikki. After fifteen minutes of exposition, brilliantly handled with conflict and humour, we have all the information we need in order to realise that the story isn't about what Pat wants but what he needs, which is to get better and move on from Nikki. We don't know less than the protagonist, we know more, and that allows us to fully identify with him over the rest of the story.

So it's usually a good thing to limit exposition to the minimum, but don't fall into the opposite trap which is to make a mystery when the audience really needs more information in order to be able to understand the situation, the characters and their decisions. Identification is closely linked to the way information is managed, so it's crucial to find the right balance for exposition: getting rid of the unnecessary, for example backstory needed for character design rather than for story comprehension, but conveying, ideally through visual storytelling rather than dialogue, what we do need to know about the characters' past in order to be emotionally involved in the story.

Solutions

Let's recap and see how we can address this note.

✓   One obvious solution is to **reduce the amount of exposition** to the minimum needed to tell the story. The audience doesn't have to be told everything. We can piece things together as the story unfolds. We don't need to know every detail about the characters' past. Some writers do a lot of work on their characters' backstory, and they might think that this information is meant to be shared. But this is a mistake. This work is mostly needed for character design, so that their actions, decisions and aspirations are coherent. So keep the design to yourself, and use it to write consistent, three-dimensional characters. Don't bore us with their backstory, unless this information is critical in terms of understanding the situation, the characters' decisions, their emotions or their actions.

✓   **We don't need to be told everything upfront**. Many writers sense that exposition is dull, so they try to get rid of it early in the story, which often leads to a boring dramatic Act 1. Or a slow pilot / first episode in a TV series that is likely to end up on the virtual editing room floor. Instead, consider spreading exposition throughout the story, trying to turn each bit of information into an interesting plot-point: a surprise, a new way for the protagonist to reach the goal, a new obstacle – anything that creates conflict. You might also consider starting the story in the middle or towards the end of the action, with a *teaser flashback*, so that you can take a bit more time to introduce your characters and the situation after you've delivered this strong hook. This is what *Breaking Bad*, *Goodfellas*, *The Hangover* and many other successful stories do, to avoid starting with a long expository first act before the audience has a reason to keep watching. An efficient teaser often sets up an interesting question, usually through a mystery or dramatic irony.

✓ **Avoid artificial situations and clichés.** Sometimes, one character tells another something they already know. This feels artificial because although it looks like the characters are talking to each other, they are really talking to the audience, as a way to convey exposition. You want to avoid this at all costs, but ideally without using one of the many clichés, such as the friend who comes back after a long trip that a character has to fill in. You really have to be inventive with the devices you use to convey exposition.

✓ **Use conflict to entertain the audience.** Because exposition is boring, try to draw us in with conflict (the character who provides the information doesn't want to talk, or the character who receives it doesn't want to hear it) or entertain us with comedy (every gag is conflict). If you make it dramatic, moving or funny, exposition becomes a lot more palatable. Be careful though not to distract our attention so much with conflict that we don't pay attention to the information itself. For this reason, it's better if the conflict, serious or not, is connected to the exposition.

There is a great example of a well-handled exposition scene at the beginning of *Aliens*. As for any sequel, you want the story to be understandable and enjoyable for the fraction of the audience that hasn't seen the first instalment. So Ripley is invited to join the rescue mission as a "consultant", and is asked to brief the trigger-happy G.I.s who are supposed to help find the colonists who have vanished from LV-431. As she starts to tell them what happened in *Alien*, she faces two strong conflicts: first, she has to retell traumatic events, the nature of the information is conflictual, and she struggles to find the words. Second, they don't take her seriously, and that means conflict for Ripley, but also for the G.I.s because we know something that they don't: Aliens are not to be underestimated. This dramatic irony (the audience knows something that at least one character is unaware of) is another element often used in sequels that helps to generate conflict in the scene.

As you can see, we have a perfect combination to make this exposition scene palatable: the nature of the information is conflictual, the character who has to provide the information doesn't really want to and those on the receiving end don't take it seriously, when we know that they should. This scene does the job of bringing those who haven't seen the first instalment up to speed, but far from being boring for those who have seen *Alien*, it actually draws them in emotionally because they know the G.I.s are making a mistake that they're going to regret.

✓ If you're struggling with reducing the amount of exposition, **consider starting the story earlier.** That way, you can open the story with what happened in the past, and then jump to present time once you've shown the past events.

✓ If that doesn't work or isn't appropriate, start the story in present time, then when you need to convey the information about past events to the audience, **consider using a flashback as an alternative to exposition.** That way, instead of having a character telling us about past events, we go back in the past to actually see them, then come back to present time and resume the action. This is a legitimate use of flashbacks. Just make sure you don't overdo it.

✓ If you need multiple flashbacks and can't find a way around it, **check that your different timeframes are properly structured**, so that we don't feel like the action stops every time we go to the past. Using flashbacks or even a flashback structure can be a great way to limit exposition, but it shouldn't be an excuse for a confusing story. You still want the audience to be emotionally involved in both stories. Ideally, you want the past-time action to move the present-time action forward, and the present-time action to inform the past-time action. This is what happens in *True Detective*, *The Secret in Their Eyes*, *The Bridges of Madison County*, *Citizen Kane*, *Amadeus*, and other flashback-oriented films. Certainly some memorable stories use a flashback structure, but they can be very hard to pull off. For one successful exception, there are hundreds of failed ones. This is why reading the word FLASHBACK in a script triggers alarm bells in experienced readers, so beware!

Connected Problems in This Book
- 31 The Drama / Conflict Is Told But Not Shown
- 27 The Script Is Cold, Unemotional
- 03 The Story Takes Too Long to Start
- 35 The Script Is Unnecessarily Complex

Sections in Screenwriting Unchained
- 'A Good Set-up', 'Cold Start' and 'Flashbacks: To FB or Not to FB' in 2.3 Craft the Draft
- 'Visual Storytelling' and 'Planting and Pay-Off' in 2.1 Behind the Scenes

Sections in 12 Ways to a Stronger Screenplay
- Set-Up / Story World
- Managing Information (Who Knows What When?)
- Planting, Pay-Off and Visual Storytelling

31 The Drama / Conflict Is Told But Not Shown

Sometimes there is a reason why we can't show certain events. For example, in a sitcom or a no-budget / micro-budget feature, you might not have the resources to change location or to show what's happening because it would simply be too costly to move the cast and crew outside of the studio or to show that fire raging outside or that tornado destroying everything.

But if we set this specific budgetary constraint aside, it's usually a good idea to show rather than tell because film (and TV) is a visual medium. This applies to both small and big events in a story.

For example, can you find a way to show how a character learns something important, other than having another character telling them? Usually, this kind of visual storytelling is achieved with planting and pay-off, a way to assign a specific meaning to an element, be it an object, a character, a location, a song. When the audience sees or hears it again, they understand its significance.

One of the most famous examples of visual storytelling can be seen in *The Apartment*. Protagonist C.C. Baxter doesn't know that his boss is having fun in Baxter's own apartment with Fran Kubelik, the woman Baxter loves. He makes this connection when he sees Fran using a broken mirror that he knows belongs to Sheldrake's mistress. This shocking moment for him is also the resolution of a strong dramatic irony (we knew that Fran was Sheldrake's mistress, Baxter didn't). Thanks to visual storytelling, this conflict is shown without any dialogue, which makes it more powerful.

Focusing on visual storytelling works at scene or sequence level, but it also works at story level in order to show rather than tell. Remember, drama means action: protagonists have to be able to *do* something about the story problem, rather than talk about it.

For example, if you look at the overall design of your story, does it describe a main dramatic *action*, something that the protagonist has to consciously *do* in order to try to resolve an external problem, as would be the case in a **plot-led story**?

Or do your protagonist's actions cause a main dramatic *evolution*, something that the protagonist has to unconsciously *change* to resolve an internal problem, as would be the case in a **character-led story**?

Or does your story weave together many storylines connected to the same theme, each of them structured as a plot-led or character-led strand, forming a multi-stranded narrative, as would be the case in a **theme-led story**?

All of these are valid ways to develop dramatic actions that *show* what the protagonist(s) do, as they try to resolve – consciously or not – the story problem.

Or – and this is when this note might pop up – does your script convey an episodic story that is instead narrated through a series of devices, such as letters, voiceovers and characters talking about events or about their feelings?

This is more likely to be the case if you're working on the adaptation of a novel or other literary material that might be designed to convey internal thoughts or emotions to the reader through the internal voice of characters. Literature can do this very well. It's one of the most pleasurable elements of a well-written novel: having the ability to share the internal thoughts, feelings and emotions of a character through a direct channel – the written page.

Screenplays don't work like this. They can achieve a strong emotional connection, but it's through identification caused by understanding conflict experienced by a character as we witness it, rather than through being told about it.

So if you come from a literary background, you might need to shift your approach. Instead of having characters talk about their feelings and emotions, or a narrator explaining to us what they think, what they feel, and why, you'll look for ways to dramatise this. Can you design situations that *show* the characters experiencing conflict and so feeling emotions? Then, though the identification link that you've created between the protagonist and the audience, can you get the audience to share these emotions?

This note could also be related to another common problem: <u>30</u> <u>The Script Contains Too Much Exposition</u>, so you might want to take a look at that as well.

Solutions

Overall, here is how you can address this problem:

✓ If your work is an adaptation of existing material, **check that your script isn't still a novel or a theatre play, superficially formatted like a screenplay.** These art forms tend to rely on dialogue (theatre) or internal thoughts (novels). Adapting them isn't only about cutting them down if they are too long or deciding who the main character is. It's about making them work for a different medium: the screen, small or big. This often means you're going to have to design a main dramatic action or evolution if not present, or find a way to make the story work as a theme-led story, hybrid or exception. There is a great deal of design involved in an adaptation in order to make the story work for the screen.

✓ **Look for tell-tale signs of a literary origin**: letters, diaries or voiceovers are devices often used in literature but when the story is adapted to screen, it's rare to see them work as well. Scorsese pulls off a voiceover in *Goodfellas*, but that's the exception rather than the rule. If you think you've found a way to make these literary devices work in your screenplay, great, but if you have any doubt, take a hard look at your work and see if it needs more dramatisation and more visual storytelling.

✓ Verify that **important pieces of information in your story are conveyed visually** whenever possible, especially those related to managing information: mystery, surprise but also setting up or resolving a dramatic irony, i.e. when you tell the audience something that at least one character isn't aware of, or when that character, the victim of the dramatic irony, finds out. This is usually achieved using planting and pay-off: a specific meaning is assigned to an element in the story, so that when it pays off later we can visually convey the information that leads to a conflict, as in the example from *The Apartment*. In general, dramatic irony is a key tool to master in order to show conflict rather than telling it, because it can be set up, exploited and resolved visually. This is why it's used so often. You can read more about this in *Screenwriting Unchained*. Download a free sampler in <u>If You Want to Find Out More...</u>

✓ This also applies to backstory. **Can you find a way to encapsulate visually what the audience needs to know about a character's past**, instead of having characters telling us about their past? This might mean showing a key past event at the beginning of the film instead of relying on exposition to tell the audience about it later. It could also mean finding something visual (a scar, a picture, a location) that gives us the essence of what we need to know about them. For example, in the opening sequence of *Rear Window*, Hitchcock shows us photographs of a car accident on a race track. When we meet photographer Jeff Jefferies at the end of this travelling shot, we realise that he's the one who's taken the pictures, and they are the reason why he's stuck in a wheelchair with a broken leg. This is great visual storytelling.

✓ **Choose your weapon**. For example, if a secondary character (not the protagonist) finds out about something we knew but they didn't, it's fine to resolve this dramatic irony through dialogue. But when the victim of a dramatic irony is the protagonist, consider using visual storytelling to resolve it in order to achieve maximum emotional impact. For example, in *The Apartment*, Fran Kubelik is also victim of a dramatic irony. She doesn't know that Sheldrake has no intention of divorcing his wife, but we do. When she finds out, it is through dialogue, with Mrs. Olson, Sheldrake's secretary. This is fine because Fran isn't the protagonist. However, when Baxter, the protagonist, finds out a bit later that Fran is Sheldrake's mistress, using visual storytelling this time, the emotional impact of the moment is much stronger. You don't have to use visual storytelling all the time. It's about using it when it matters, and as often as possible.

Connected Problems in This Book

- 30 The Script Contains Too Much Exposition
- 09 The Screenplay Is Too Dry or Not Visual Enough
- 11 The Screenplay Is Written Like a Novel

Sections in Screenwriting Unchained

- 'Visual Storytelling' and 'Planting and Pay-Off' in 2.1 Behind the Scenes

Sections in 12 Ways to a Stronger Screenplay

- Managing Conflict (Who Wants / Needs What and Why?)
- Managing Information (Who Knows What When?)
- Planting, Pay-Off and Visual Storytelling

32 The Script Privileges Style Over Substance

When you get this note, it usually means you've focused too much on how you're telling the story, and not enough on the story itself. It's important to have a voice, but not if it drowns out everything else.

In your screenplay, you might be concentrating on its style, on how innovative, different or challenging it is, but you could be losing sight of its main function, which is to deliver a meaningful, moving and entertaining story. Screenwriting isn't about creating something that has never been done before (although it does occasionally happen). It's about creating something that has been done a thousand times, yet making it look fresh and original.

So focus on the story, on the characters, on the universality of their conflicts and emotions, and you'll be halfway towards zapping this note into oblivion.

Solutions

Here are a few more elements to consider:

✓ **Dialogue**. Are your jokes all in a particular style, leading to all the characters speaking with the same voice? Or are all of your characters different versions of yourself, trying to hammer the same theme? Instead of using characters as substitutes for yourself, try to write dialogue that pays off a situation or a characterisation, so that if they are funny or meaningful, it's down to context rather than style. If a line is just as funny when you take it out of the context of the script, you might consider rewriting it. It should be funny because of who said it, why or when they said it, or what effect it has. Not because it's funny in itself. There are exceptions of course, but "Well, nobody's perfect", one of the best toppers in film history, isn't as funny, clever or meaningful if you haven't seen *Some Like It Hot*.

✓ **Technical directions.** You might have a very clear idea of how you'd want to shoot your screenplay, but unless you're directing it and this is a shooting script meant for the crew, no one wants to read about shot sizes, camera angles or transitions. This is distracting and often off-putting. It won't only distract the reader, it will also annoy the director and the actors, who don't like to be told how to do their work (just as writers don't like to be told how to do theirs). So unless it's absolutely key to the situation, don't write how a scene should be shot or how a line should be said. Concentrate on your job as a writer, which is the design of a story meant for the screen. If you need a close up, there are many ways to suggest one without ever writing these words in the script, for example by describing a detail that could only be seen in a close-up: a mole, a small scar or tattoo, an earring, an inscription on a photograph, etc.

✓ **Unnecessary flashbacks, gimmicky multi-stranded narrative, confusing non-linear narrative**. No creative writer wants to follow a formula, and the audience doesn't want that either. However, if straying away from convention means that your story isn't delivering what it's meant to (characters your audience cares about and a riveting plot), then you might have to change tack. Make your characters original. Find universal challenges and emotions. Design original situations. Strive for simplicity, and if you need complexity, make sure it doesn't bring confusion. Disappear behind your characters, and let *them* show how original you are. More on this in 35 The Script Is Unnecessarily Complex.

✓ **"Knowing" voice.** Remember that ultimately your audience isn't your reader. If you tell your story winking at people from the film world or making inside jokes, you are likely to alienate your potential audience, unless this is an additional layer on top of a story that works for those who won't get these references. An astute reader will identify this and might comment that the script privileges style over substance. So, again, focus on the essence of the story: the characters, the conflict, the emotions, the dramatic situations that you design. Write with humility, design with purpose and give your characters more space to blossom and capture our imagination.

✓ **Literary writing style.** You might also write in a literary way – using long sentences, adverbs, descriptions of the thoughts or feelings of the characters, long descriptions of locations, poetic style. All this has little place in a screenplay, which, unlike a novel, an essay or a poem, isn't the end product. It's only a blueprint for the actual creation. The quality of the writing, from a literary point of view, weighs in at around zero percent in the value of the finished product. Apart from the dialogue, none of this writing will remain. Of course the writing style is important in a screenplay, but it usually focuses on adverb-free, short sentences – becoming even shorter in action scenes – and the ability to convey a visual action in each paragraph. So you might want to explore a few of the connected problems listed below if you think that you might be suffering from "literary-itis".

✓ **Hectic action style.** Almost the opposite of the previous situation, this is pushing the idea that a script should be all about visual storytelling to the extreme, leaving us nothing but noise and flashes of light. In an action movie, we do need well-crafted set pieces, but if we don't care about the characters, they'll be as boring to read as they'll be to watch, no matter how many CGI special effects and stunts you plan to throw on the screen. It's great if you're thinking visually, but you might need to take some of your focus away from the plot and from groovy action scenes. Even in *Mad Max: Fury Road*, the characters are developed so that we care about what happens to them. So have you taken the time to introduce your characters? Do we know enough about them to feel that they are real people? Are they original yet still relatable? Similarly, is your story about something, or is it purely a plot-led chase? Often, characters and theme are the substance that is missing when you get this note. Instead of focusing purely on the plot (what happens), think about who it's happening to, and why.

Connected Problems in This Book

- 11 The Screenplay Is Written Like a Novel
- 21 There Is Too Much Dialogue
- 35 The Script Is Unnecessarily Complex
- 40 The Premise Is an Artificial Excuse For Action

Sections in Screenwriting Unchained

- 'Visual Storytelling' and 'Planting and Pay-Off' in 2.1 Behind the Scenes
- 'Flashbacks: To FB or Not to FB?' in 2.3 Craft the Draft

Sections in 12 Ways to a Stronger Screenplay

- Managing Conflict (Who Wants/Needs What and Why?)
- Managing Information (Who Knows What When?)
- Planting, Pay-Off and Visual Storytelling

33 The Tone of the Script Is Unclear

When this note shows up, it usually means the reader is not sure how seriously they're supposed to take the story. Perhaps it was presented as a serious drama or a thriller, but comedic elements undermine the overall tone, which confuses the reader / viewer. Mixing genres isn't always a problem. For example, horror and comedy go well together, but sometimes finding the right balance can be tricky.

If the reader thinks they are dealing with a light comedy, and it ends with the abrupt death of the protagonist, it's certainly shocking, and not in a good way, because nothing prepared the reader for such an ending.

Another example: the reader thought the story was realistic, and suddenly science-fiction, paranormal or fantasy elements are introduced. Or vice-versa: The reader was engrossed in a fantasy or sci-fi thriller and midway, some mundane, realistic elements are brought in, leading to a very down-to-earth conclusion. This rarely works either.

Why?

This is mostly because telling a story is like inviting the audience to play a game with you. In order to get them to participate, you tell them the rules of the game, and either they say "okay, I'm in", or "sorry, not for me". Once you've got them on board, you can't change the rules of the game without causing some disappointment, confusion or even a feeling of betrayal in the most extreme cases.

Solutions

So when you get this note, look at these potential issues:

✓   **If the story fits more than one genre, are these genres compatible?** For example, comedy / horror tends to work well, but comedy / thriller is harder to pull off as the comedy often undermines the thriller element.

✓   **Have you clearly defined the rules of the story world you're exploring, and are you sticking to them?** When you start telling a story, you define a story world with its own rules, and you sign a contract with the audience. Don't break it! More on this in 36 The Supernatural Element Is Too Vague.

✓   **If you use humour in an otherwise serious story, have you timed it well?** Humour can bring welcome relief during or after a very tense sequence, but get the timing wrong and it can ruin the moment and even the story.

✓   **If you bring dark tones into an otherwise light story, is this shift in tone planted earlier in the story?** Are there elements in the story that prepare the audience to accept that it's not as light as it seems? In *Life is Beautiful*, a darker subplot becomes the main plot, although not all audiences of that film accepted the significant shift in tone, even with the "rise of fascism" subplot being present in the first half of the story.

✓   **Is your ending satisfying?** The question is never whether the ending is happy or unhappy, as both can be satisfying depending on how the story is designed, but roughly do the characters deserve the end they meet? The audience has a strong sense of justice, and we tend to rebel when we feel that the protagonist meets an undeserved ending (be it positive or negative), because if we spend two hours identifying with a character, we become the character.

So if the character gets punished because of mistakes they've made or failed to correct (what most tragic stories are about), we can accept that. But if we feel that they've tried hard and they've made the right decisions, then they fail or die, we're bound to feel short-changed. This is especially the case if there is no value in that death, for example if it doesn't serve the greater good, which is what most heroic stories are about. Overall, the audience is just as likely to reject an unnecessarily dark conclusion as we are to feel let down by an artificial happy ending. More on this in 10 The Ending Doesn't Work.

✓ **If your story is plot-led, have you found a way to develop a character arc that is connected to the plot but doesn't take it over?** If you let character evolution take over in plot-led stories, it can give the feeling that the tone is unclear.

In most plot-led stories, what you want is a character who needs to grow, not necessarily to change, so there is no need to have backstories with such dark undertones. Sometimes, an internal obstacle is all you need, and it doesn't have to be resolved by the end of the story. Chief Brody is afraid of water in *Jaws*, and although he has to confront that fear during the climax, he might then find it even less appealing to get back in the sea after his ordeal.

Sometimes, the main growth is the evolution of the relationship between two main characters, for example in a buddy movie. Finding the right backstory and evolution for your protagonist in a plot-led story is key to getting the tone right. Don't think that they necessarily have to go through a life-changing transformation. That's not the point. For example, in *The Heat*, Sandra Bullock's character is lonely and stuck up. She doesn't have to overcome a huge childhood trauma. That's the right level of evolution for an action buddy comedy. The evolution is there to make the story more interesting and give more depth to the character, but it's the gravy, not the main course. The core of the film, as with most buddy movies, is the evolution of the *relationship* between the two characters, how they hate each other initially but complement each other and end up best friends. Not necessarily how one of them overcomes a personal trauma.

✓ **If your story is character-led, you might want to look at the protagonist's problem on the plot side of the story and see where it lies in Maslow's Hierarchy of Needs.** (If you're not familiar with this, please read Is Maslow Running the Show? at the beginning of *Screenwriting Unchained*). If the problem on the plot side sits lower than the problem on the character side, make sure that this isn't causing some confusion regarding what's really at stake in the story. For example, if you want to design a story where the main character needs to change the way they relate to women, don't then put their life in danger because that might make us feel unsure of what the story is about. Survival, if expected to be taken seriously in the story, will most likely take over a need for love or intimacy. There are no rules, but being aware of this can help you ensure that the way you design the plot doesn't undermine the main evolution, which is the backbone of the script in a character-led story. Otherwise, the stakes might be unclear, which can lead to this note.

Connected Problems in This Book

- 08 The Story Is Confusing
- 10 The Ending Doesn't Work
- 36 The Supernatural Element Is Too Vague

Sections in Screenwriting Unchained

- 1.3 Is Maslow Running the Show?
- 'Genre', 'A Good Set-Up', 'Story World', 'Theme' and 'Happy Ending vs Satisfying Ending' in 2.3 Craft the Draft

Sections in 12 Ways to a Stronger Screenplay

- Story-Type and Genre
- M-Factor (What's at Stake)
- Theme (What Is the Story About?)
- Set-up / Story World
- Satisfying Ending

34 Too Many Questions Are Left Unanswered

Screenwriting isn't an exact science, but if you remember your maths lessons – sorry to bring back unpleasant memories for many – whenever you open a parenthesis in an equation there should be a matching closing one, otherwise the equation is unbalanced. It's very similar in a story.

When you raise our interest with a question, we expect to get an answer or an explanation by the end of the story. Mystery, for example can be a great hook because we don't like unanswered questions, so we want to find out the resolution. Cliffhangers work well too because leaving the protagonist facing an unresolved conflict – or hearing an unexpected piece of news that changes everything – without knowing what's going to happen next is tantalising. But this comes at a cost: when using these devices, you make a promise, which means that you have to deliver answers at some point, otherwise you create disappointment, frustration or confusion.

Solutions

So let's see which usual suspects trigger this note, and how each of them can be addressed:

✓ **Unanswered dramatic questions**. This is one of the main hooks you're going to use to focus the audience's interest during the story: what the protagonist wants or needs over the whole film, over a dramatic sequence, over a scene. As soon as we understand who needs or wants what and why in a story, you raise a dramatic question. We want to know what's going to happen next because we want to find out if the protagonist reaches the goal or finds a way to change.

Usually, an answer to the main dramatic question is provided during the climax of the film. But smaller dramatic questions are raised in many sequences, scenes, subplots or strands. Fail to answer some of these, and this can lead to frustration. So the best way to remedy this is to go through your story, list every time you raise a dramatic question (Who wants or needs what and why?) in a scene, sequence, subplot or strand, and make sure that you answer that question, or if you don't that it's not a cause for confusion. Open endings can work (for example in *Birdman*, see below), but only if the audience can come up with their own, personal answer, feel sure of it and are convinced that the filmmaker meant them to come to that conclusion. In other words, not being at odds with the meaning of the film.

✓ **Unanswered ironic questions**. This one is less well-known, but it nevertheless happens. Have you forgotten to resolve one or more dramatic ironies in the story? A dramatic irony is when the audience knows something that at least one character – the victim of the dramatic irony – doesn't know. This is exploited over a scene, a sequence, sometimes the whole film, and we expect the resolution: we want to see how the victim will react when they find out. Instead of or besides a *dramatic* question (Will the protagonist reach their goal?) we have one or more ironic questions: How and when will the victim of the dramatic irony find out?

In some stories, for example in *Tootsie*, most of the characters are victims of a dramatic irony over the whole film. We know that Michael Dorsey is a man pretending to be a woman and we want to see the characters' reaction when they realise that Dorothy Michaels isn't a woman.

So did you forget to resolve one or more dramatic ironies in your story? If you have, is it a problem or not? For example, in *Back to the Future*, Marty's parents never find out that the teenage boy that made them an item in the past was their son. This unresolved dramatic irony isn't a problem because there are other pay-offs at the end – in fact, resolving it would weaken the ending. But it could be an issue in another story. Imagine, for example, if the flower girl at the end of *City Lights* never realised that the man who gave her the money for her eye operation, the man she thought was a generous millionaire, was actually a penniless tramp. Or if Roxane in *Cyrano de Bergerac* never discovered that it wasn't Christian who wrote these love letters, but Cyrano. Or if none of the characters in *Tootsie* found out that Dorothy Michaels wasn't a woman.

✓ **Unanswered thematic questions.** What is your story about? At some point in the narrative, maybe we thought we knew, so we were expecting this to be explored, but nothing or not enough is delivered, so we're puzzled. Or perhaps we thought the story was about one thing, but the climax answers a different question. Can the ending still be satisfying? If we're unsure what the story was about, we can't help but wonder if the writer had a handle on it. If you think this might be an issue in your story, check that your main dramatic action / evolution explores a problem connected to the story theme, so that its conclusion brings an answer to your thematic question.

✓ **Open endings.** We have an open ending when we don't know for sure if the character succeeds or fails, lives or dies, gets to change or not. In other words, we don't know how the story ends. Given that the ending of a story conveys most of its meaning, this can be very frustrating. Sometimes, it's fine because although we don't know for sure, we know enough to make up our own ending and that's part of the pleasure delivered by the story: in *Birdman* for example, we're all free to interpret the ending in our own way. Riggan jumping out of the window and his daughter smiling, looking up rather than down, is ambiguous without being confusing.

Other times, the actual ending isn't shown, but there is little doubt left. For example, at the end of *Thelma & Louise*, the car and our protagonists freeze mid-air, but there is no doubt about the outcome. So if you do want an open ending because you feel it's more appropriate, can you make sure that it's still satisfying?

✓ **Should you consider a theme-led story?** Sometimes you struggle to provide a "closed" ending because you can't find a satisfying one. This could be because your story explores a problem in society that can't be solved. In this case, you might want to consider making your story **theme-led**. Instead of having to make a decision about whether the problem is solved or not for a single protagonist – which might feel unrealistic or depressing – why not explore the same problem through a multi-stranded narrative, and give each of the strands a different ending, some positive, some negative? This won't feel as definitive as a main plot carrying most of the meaning through a single ending, yet the combined endings of all the strands might convey an overall optimistic or pessimistic point of view about this problem in society.

✓ **Have you forgotten to tie up subplots in a plot-led or character-led story, or strands in a theme-led story?** Sometimes a writer not only forgets to bring a dramatic answer to a subplot, a sequence or a strand, they simply drop it altogether. A character disappears, a dramatic action or evolution vanishes entirely and the reader is at a loss – especially if that reader is particularly attached to or interested in that part of the story. So make sure you close every story element in the script.

✓ **Do you have a point of view about the problem explored in the story?** Sometimes questions are left unanswered not because you forgot about them, or because you've struggled to find the right ending, but because you don't have a point of view about the situation, the theme and the emotions that the story explores. If you don't care enough, or if you feel ambivalent about the problem or the characters, the audience will sense it and might be put off by it. So ask yourself what your take is on the story problem and revisit the narrative to make sure that the way you explore this problem – and, more importantly, bring it to a conclusion – conveys a clear viewpoint.

Connected Problems in This Book

- 35 The Script Is Unnecessarily Complex
- 22 The Ending Is an Anti-Climax
- 10 The Ending Doesn't Work
- 38 The Plot Is Contrived
- 23 The Ending Is a *Deus Ex Machina*
- 17 The Script Loses the Plot in the Third Act

Sections in Screenwriting Unchained

- 'Happy Ending vs Satisfying Ending' in 2.3 Craft the Draft

Sections in 12 Ways to a Stronger Screenplay

- Satisfying Ending

35 The Script Is Unnecessarily Complex

The fairly recent trend towards non-linear narrative and other experimental story structures has made this issue more prevalent. Sometimes the note is entirely justified, sometimes it's not.

Let's first talk about this trend, the reasons behind it and whether having a complex story is a good thing or a bad thing.

Over the last few decades, mainstream story structure theory has become more and more prescriptive. The way the *dramatic* three-act structure has been reduced by screenwriting gurus to a superficial *logistical* three-act structure is the main reason creative writers have been tempted to free themselves from it.

When you're talented and want to write an original piece, you believe – and rightly so – that there is more to screenwriting than three acts of fixed length, a midpoint and mandatory plot points for all stories.

Some have tried to move beyond this simplistic paradigm by suggesting more acts – four, five, seven – or more mandatory elements – eight sequences, fifteen beats, twenty-two steps, etc. Any arbitrary number sounding like "enough" to steer away from the limitation of a logistical three-act structure, i.e. a superficial structure based on minutes or page numbers.

Unfortunately, most of these attempts were just as prescriptive, if not more, and were still piggy-backing on the logistical three-act structure, never really freeing the writer from its oppressive diktat. They were still focusing on a mandatory story *format* rather than a flexible story *structure*, as explained in 19 The Script Feels Formulaic.

So a natural evolution was to try to break from single protagonist and linear storytelling and to go multi-stranded or non-linear.

Although this approach is not new, it has certainly become more and more fashionable over the last decade, and some filmmakers have embraced this with considerable success.

This reaction, while understandable, is a solution to a problem that doesn't really exist. The logistical three-act structure is a fairly recent dogmatic approach and it's not because it perverts the concept of story structure that the original, dramatic three-act structure itself should be thrown out like the baby with the bath water. When you fully grasp the fractal aspect of story structure, you realise that even Nolan or Haggis use the dramatic three-act structure and all the other classical tools in *Dunkirk* or *Crash*. They simply use them at strand, sequence and scene level rather than at film level.

I explain this screenwriting evolution in detail in the introduction of *Screenwriting Unchained*, so I won't go through it again here. Please see If You Want to Find Out More... at the end of this book for a download link to a free sampler (first fifty pages).

How to identify whether a story is unnecessarily complex or not?

The first thing you want to check is whether your "unnecessarily complex story" achieves its main objective, which is to move, entertain, and provide meaning to an audience.

If it does, your complex story might be an exception. It might be more difficult to get it financed in a risk-adverse climate, but that doesn't mean that it can't blossom into something wonderful. There is definitely an appetite from the audience for "different stories". This is mainly caused by the kind of predictability induced by the prescriptive formats mentioned above, when the same thing happens in every single script at the same page number, whether it's a "Refusal of the Call" or an "All is Lost" moment (don't worry if you're not familiar with these terms).

There is nothing wrong with a complex story if it still delivers meaning, entertainment and emotion. Stories like *Dunkirk, Crash, Inception, Source Code, Memento, Birdman, The Secret in Their Eyes, L.A. Confidential* and *Cloud Atlas* are complex, unconventionally structured stories that find an audience, even if it's not always a wide audience. Keeping the budget reasonable certainly improves your chances of getting this kind of story off the ground, especially if you're a newcomer. *Memento* was hard to finance for Nolan despite its low budget and despite it being his second feature. *Inception* would have probably been much more difficult to green light before *The Dark Knight*. Getting Warner to finance the $150M World War II multi-stranded, non-linear epic *Dunkirk* on a 76-page script would be an impossible feat for any filmmaker without the impressive string of box-office successes that Nolan had secured on his track record by then: *The Prestige, The Dark Knight, Inception, The Dark Knight Rises, Interstellar*. It took Nolan more than twenty years to get *Dunkirk* made (he started developing the concept in 1992, before *Memento*). So try to be realistic: a complex story can make producers and distributors nervous.

For every successful exception, there are hundreds of failed ones that miss the target because they might be complex but don't deliver enough meaning, entertainment and emotion. Or they don't get made because the filmmakers don't have the track record needed to command the film's budget.

So as a first step, if you have designed a complex structure because you felt frustrated with prescriptive formats and wanted to try something different and if you feel it's not working, you might want to consider telling your story more classically – for example, going back to a linear narrative with a main dramatic action or evolution – while still using a more flexible approach to story structure. This is what the Story-Type Method is about. The *logistical* three-act structure and all its cookie-cutter derivatives are simplistic. But leaving the *dramatic* three-act structure behind won't necessarily add complexity to your project. It often brings confusion, which leads to a diminished emotional involvement from the audience.

Here's a question to help you make this decision: Is the complex design an integral part of your story concept (as in *Source Code, Inception, Groundhog Day, Memento*)? If it is non-linear, for example, do you need the non-linearity to make your point, because that's part of the theme, tightly connected to the meaning of the story (*The Secret in Their Eyes, Cloud Atlas*), or is it a "gimmick"? It's usually when it's the latter that you'll get this note. When the non-linearity or the complexity of the story is tied to its concept, it becomes more difficult to criticise, provided the story works.

What's most important here is to make the distinction between complexity and confusion, and between simplicity and being simplistic. You don't want your story to be simplistic, but making it confusing isn't an improvement. Simplicity is one of the most difficult things to achieve in storytelling, yet when it's attained it can provide the most powerful, moving, beautiful stories. If you want your story to be complex, do it for the right reasons, and make sure that it still delivers meaning, entertainment and emotion. This is what well-designed multi-stranded narratives and hybrids or exceptions manage to achieve.

Solutions

To sum it up, here's how to address this note:

✓   **Assess if it's making a valid point.** Some stories need to be complex because they explore a complex concept. Others are so focused on a superficial, flashy structure that they leave behind more important elements. If there is a conceptual need for your story to be complex, make sure that it still delivers meaning, entertainment and emotion. If there is no reason for it except the need to "try something different", then consider exploring more efficient ways to tell your story, which of course doesn't mean it has to become less original.

✓   **If the main motivation for having a complex story structure is rejecting the dogmatic, prescriptive, *logistical* three-act structure, think again.** The *dramatic* three-act structure can be used not only over the whole story but also for its parts, whether they are dramatic acts, sequences, scenes, subplots or strands. This provides a lot more flexibility than a logistical approach tied to page numbers or minutes, and allows you to explore various story-types (plot-led, character-led, theme-led as well as hybrids or exceptions) before exploring the nuclear option, which is going non-linear. I cover this in detail in the introduction and first chapter of *Screenwriting Unchained*.

✓   **If you decide to go for a non-linear or multi-stranded story structure, make sure that you structure each** storyline in such a way that the audience is able to follow them and remain emotionally involved. A multi-stranded narrative (many strands and no main plot), a non-linear narrative (different storylines taking place in more than one timeline) or any combination (such as a non-linear, multi-stranded narrative) can fail to engage the audience if each part isn't well-structured and sufficiently connected to the others. It's easy to write a confusing narrative that doesn't work. It's far more difficult to deliver a working exception: a complex narrative that still delivers meaning, entertainment and emotion. There is whole chapter on the different types of flashbacks and how to handle a flashback structure in *Screenwriting Unchained*, so it could be a good idea to explore this further if it applies to your story. The chapters on Developing a Theme-Led Story and Developing Something Else: Hybrids and Exceptions might also provide further alternatives.

✓   **Another way to look at it: Decide if you want to get rid of "unnecessarily" or "complex" in order to address the note.** There is nothing wrong with a complex story if it works. So to get rid of the "unnecessarily", you have to make sure that the story concept itself requires a complex narrative, whether it's non-linear, multi-stranded or something else. You also have to check that the complex story still delivers the right mix of meaning, entertainment and emotion for its intended audience. The alternative is to get rid of the "complex", when complex means confusing, gimmicky, or form over substance. In that case, what the note means is that the artificial complexity of the story gets in the way of delivering a far more efficient screenplay. Ditching the artificial complexity might be the way to improve the story, and it's possible to achieve this without making it conventional or predictable (which no good story should be). For example, working on managing conflict and managing information, especially using dramatic irony (when the audience knows something that at least one character is unaware of), can lead to complex stories such as *The Lives of Others* or *The Departed*.

✓   **If your story is complex, has to remain complex and if you believe that it works in an unconventional way, then be ready to fight for it, and be clever about the way you go about it**. The person delivering the note might not be the right partner to move the project further. In that case, especially if you're a newcomer, check that the budget is coherent with the potential audience for the film, especially if there is no cast attached. It's unlikely that *Cloud Atlas* would have been made without Tom Hanks, even with the Wachowskis attached. It's a complex, unconventional story that required a high budget, which makes recouping the investment far less likely without a stellar cast.

This doesn't necessarily mean that complex, unconventional narratives can only be made if they are low-budget or no-budget, only that you will save your energy and will increase the chances of getting the project made if you take all of the parameters into account. The more complex the story, the more you'll have to prove its viability. Development finance becomes less likely if you're not an established talent, and even production finance will be more difficult to attract unless other elements (director, cast) give investors the feeling that they can mitigate the increased perceived risk. Green-lighting a project is never solely about the script. It's a package, so taking all these elements into account can help. I explore this in more detail in Is Maslow Running the Show? in *Screenwriting Unchained*. From a screenwriting point of view, when you develop a complex story, making sure that some of its elements explore the lower levels of Maslow's Hierarchy of Needs (physiological, safety) can help widen its potential audience, hence diminish investors' resistance.

Connected Problems in This Book:
*   02 We Don't Care About the Story
*   04 The Story Is Linear, Feels Predictable
*   08 The Story Is Confusing
*   38 The Plot Is Contrived
*   39 The Theme Overshadows the Story

- 18 There Is No Clear Protagonist
- 24 There Is No Clear Antagonist
- 19 The Script Feels Formulaic
- 27 The Script Is Cold, Unemotional
- 29 The Plot Is Slowed Down By Unconnected Storylines
- 30 The Script Contains Too Much Exposition
- 32 The Script Privileges Style Over Substance

Sections in Screenwriting Unchained:
- 1.1 What's Wrong with the Three-Act Structure?
- 1.2 So What Do We Need to Get It Right?
- 1.3 Is Maslow Running the Show?
- 1.4 Hands-On: What's Your Type?
- 'Are You (or Are You Working with) an Ascending or a Descending Writer?' in 2. Developing a Plot-Led Story
- 'Managing Conflict' and 'Managing Information' in 2.1 Behind the Scenes
- 'Theme', 'Characterisation', 'Hero vs Protagonist', 'Villain vs Antagonist', 'Flashbacks: To FB or not to FB', 'Happy Ending vs Satisfying Ending' in 2.3 Craft the Draft
- 3.4 Hands-On: Growth, Change or Steadfast?
- '*Crash*' and '*Cloud Atlas*' in 4.5 Case Studies
- '*Edge of Tomorrow*', '*The Lives of Others*', '*Birdman*', '*The Secret in Their Eyes*' and '*L.A. Confidential*' in 5.5. Case Studies
- 6.2 Story Design Tools
- 'Tools, not Rules: Keep an Open Mind' in Conclusion

Sections in 12 Ways to a Stronger Screenplay:
- Story-Type and Genre
- M-Factor (What's at Stake?)
- Theme (What Is the Story About?)
- Fractal Aspect of Story Structure
- Managing Conflict (Who Wants / Needs What and Why?)
- Managing Information (Who Knows What When?)
- Character (Change, Growth or Steadfast?)
- Antagonist or Catalyst: Who is Testing your Protagonist?
- Satisfying Ending

36 The Supernatural Element Is Too Vague

Sci-fi, dystopian, horror, thriller, fantasy – there are many genres that embed a supernatural element at the core of the story. When done well, this element can lead to an original or challenging story.

Unfortunately, some writers believe that they have more freedom when they are dealing with a supernatural element, which is rarely the case. In fact, it's the opposite. You have to define a clear set of rules and stick to them in order to bring coherence, believability and causality to the story.

As soon as you introduce a supernatural element to a story, you are telling the audience that your story world is extraordinary, which can be part of the appeal. The rules aren't the same as in the real world, for example when characters have super powers or when the laws of physics are bent. Or you might be asking the audience to believe in something most of us think doesn't exist in reality (ghosts, vampires, monsters, etc).

For this to work for as many people as possible, you have to get the audience to suspend disbelief.

Solutions

Here are a few tips to address this problem:

✓ **If the story doesn't take place in the real world, you need to define clear rules to make it believable.** Whether we're talking about *Harry Potter*, *The Lord of the Rings*, *Avatar*, *Divergent* or *The Maze Runner*, the rules of the world must be clearly defined and consistent. So let us know how things work in this world, with regard to physics, astronomy, society... A whole set of rules have to be defined if you want the audience to believe in your story world. And once you've made these rules clear to the audience, be sure to stick to them.

✓ **If the story takes place in the real world but you have extraordinary characters populating it, you still need to define rules and stick to them.** Just because there is a supernatural element in the story doesn't mean you can introduce new rules or powers whenever it suits you. Defining clear rules about what your extraordinary characters can and can't do is crucial to making them relatable to the audience. For example, superheroes have super powers, but they can't do everything. Often, they have a weakness that makes them vulnerable, whether it's a physical weakness (Kryptonite for Superman) or emotional (Bruce Banner's anger), otherwise it becomes difficult to get them to experience conflict and to get the audience to identify with them.

✓ **If we're talking about a supernatural power assigned to an ordinary person (or animal, as in *Rise of the Planet of the Apes*), then it might help if you define what made this possible.** It doesn't have to be possible in real life, it only has to be made plausible and explained during the set-up, so that the story doesn't immediately ask us to believe in the impossible. The fact that it happened in real life is irrelevant if it's not believable. The audience can reject something that actually happened if it's not introduced in a convincing way, and can accept something outlandish if the story sets it up properly.

✓ **Sometimes, having a character who doesn't believe in the situation – hence who is like us initially – but is convinced over time can help.** Someone in the story is asking the right questions. If the answers are convincing, then we might agree to suspend our disbelief and go along with it.

✓ **This doesn't mean that every element has to be explained, or has to be explained in detail.** Sometimes, showing that you've thought about a possible objection and have a brief answer for it is enough. In *Alien*, when someone asks Ash how his movement detecting device works, his answer is simply: "Micro-changes in air density", and everyone nods. Occasionally, a supernatural element is so exciting that there is no need to explain it, simply because we want to know what's going to happen next. This is especially the case in high-concept stories, such as *Big* or *Source Code*.

✓ **Sometimes an explanation actually weakens the story**. For example, in early drafts of *Groundhog Day*, an upset ex-girlfriend or revengeful chiromancer cast a spell on Phil Connors. This didn't add much; on the contrary, it undermined the originality of the story and its metaphorical meaning. So sometimes you have to balance the pros and cons of explaining the supernatural element. Usually, if the story makes sense emotionally, we're ready to accept almost anything (*Big, Star Wars, Groundhog Day*). It's when we can't get involved at an emotional level that we start to ask questions.

✓ **Look at the way you manage information in the story**. It's fine to start with mystery, as this can be a strong hook – we want to understand why these weird things happen – but the longer the mystery lasts, the more the audience is going to expect an intellectually satisfying answer. You might have a decent story, but a resolution to the mystery that's unsatisfying. In that case, you could look at alternative ways to manage information, for example using dramatic irony (the audience knows something that some characters are not aware of). This might make it easier to get the audience to accept the supernatural element, because we can see things or we understand things that other characters don't. Interest is raised by what we know, rather than what we don't know or understand, and that can make all the difference.

✓ **Overall, what you want to avoid at all costs is the feeling that anything can happen in the story**. We don't want a story to be predictable, and surprises are welcome, but this doesn't mean that what happens in the story shouldn't fit with the story world you have defined as well as with what has come before in the story. You might not need to explain how the main situation has started (*Big*, *Groundhog Day*), but once we've accepted the supernatural premise, you should respect the story logic. This is strongly linked to the notion of causality: cause and effect. Even in a fantasy story world, even in a story with a supernatural element, events should be caused by what's happened previously, and stem from the story world itself.

Connected Problems in This Book
- 08 The Story Is Confusing
- 33 The Tone of the Script Is Unclear
- 34 Too Many Questions Are Left Unanswered

Sections in Screenwriting Unchained
- 'Managing Information' in 2.1 Behind the Scenes
- 'Happy Ending vs. Satisfying Ending', 'A Good Set-Up' and 'Story World' in 2.3 Craft the Draft

Sections in 12 Ways to a Stronger Screenplay
- Story-Type and Genre
- Set-up / Story World
- Managing Information (Who Knows What When?)
- Satisfying Ending

37 The Protagonist Is a Conventional Hero

In order to understand this note, we first need to clarify the difference between a hero and a protagonist, as these two terms are sometimes seen as interchangeable, when they aren't.

A hero is a conceptually positive character who fights for the greater good. This can work in some stories, especially those describing heroic events or involving superheroes, but it's a restrictive definition for the central character in a story. It also focuses on the conceptually good nature of the character, which might generate sympathy (intellectual approval) but is rarely enough to generate empathy (understanding and identification). People also talk about antiheroes to overcome this limitation. I still find the notion of hero and antihero too simplistic. The world isn't black and white, and neither are protagonists.

A protagonist is the character (or group of characters sharing the same goal) experiencing the most conflict in a story, hence the character with whom we empathise. This wider definition of a protagonist helps create less conventional central characters. It's not connected to how nice the character is conceptually, or whether they are trying to achieve a positive goal or not. It's entirely related to the amount of conflict experienced by that character. If we understand the conflict, if we can relate to it, then we can feel empathy for the character even if we have no sympathy for them. This also means that we can handle conceptually negative characters as protagonists. They are often fighting an internal flaw, which leads us to empathise with them as long as they experience the most conflict in the story. More on this in <u>01 We Don't Care About the Protagonist</u>.

Solutions

So if you're getting this note, here are a few things you can look at:

✓ **Do you need a hero in your story?** Unless your central character is a positive character fighting for the greater good, you're probably after a protagonist rather than a hero. This means that you need to define which character experiences the most conflict if the story is **plot-led** (the main problem lies outside of the protagonist) or **character-led** (the main problem lies within the protagonist).

If you're dealing with a **theme-led story** (a multi-stranded narrative where the main problem often lies in society), you need to define a protagonist in as many storylines as possible, and decide whether each strand is plot-led or character-led. This is because in theme-led stories, there is no single protagonist as there is no main plot, only subplots called strands.

Hybrids and exceptions are harder to get right because it's often management of information that determines who the protagonist is. For example, the protagonist might be the victim of a strong dramatic irony (something that the audience knows but they don't), and this could be why we feel a lot of conflict for that character, rather than the more classical protagonist-goal-obstacle way of generating conflict. This is the case in stories such as *The Departed, The Lives of Others* or *The Hand That Rocks the Cradle*.

✓ **If you do need a hero, work on the design of the character to ensure that they are not conventional**. Work on their backstory and their evolution so that they don't behave, think and look like a typical hero. Think about the whole variety of gender, origin, age, psychological traits that you could use. As long as they fulfil their function, heroes don't have to be two-dimensional or stereotypical. Also, even if they behave heroically, check that they are also the protagonist, i.e. the character in the story experiencing the most conflict. This can get tricky with superheroes unless you define weaknesses (physical or emotional) that you exploit to ensure they experience conflict. This kind of internal obstacle can make them more human, without undermining the fascination caused by their power. Beware: neither a hero nor a protagonist has to change. In **plot-led stories**, which is the case for most stories involving heroes, the protagonist usually only needs to grow, because the main problem in the story lies outside of them. There is nothing fundamentally wrong with them, so they don't need to change. This unfounded rule that "the protagonist is the character who changes most in a story" often leads writers to create unnecessary traumatic backstories, which has become a convention (see the point further down about avoiding clichés).

✓ **If you don't need a hero, then work on your protagonist so that we can identify with them even if we don't like them**. Identification is about empathy, not sympathy. You don't need the audience to *like* a protagonist or approve of what they are doing. If your character is unsympathetic, you don't need to get them to save a cat to make them nicer. At the beginning of *As Good as It Gets*, Melvin Udall tries to kill his neighbour's dog because of his OCD and we soon realise that he's not only a racist but also homophobic. This is who Melvin is at the beginning of the film. His journey is about how he's going to change (as is the case in **character-led stories**). So making him nicer, in that instance, simply goes against the intention. You need the audience to *understand* your protagonist's conflict and *feel* for them. To hope for them to succeed (to reach a conscious goal in a **plot-led story** or to change in a **character-led story**) and fear that they might fail.

✓ **Hero or not hero, by all means avoid the clichéd backstory**: estranged / dead partner or children are on the top of the list, because these have been used and overused by too many action thrillers. Unless it's connected to a strong theme, as in *Gravity*, think twice before following this convention. If you have such a cliché in your story, make sure you know it's a cliché and the audience knows you know it's a cliché. Make fun of it or give it a new spin, as in *John Wick*, where the clichéd dead wife sends a puppy as a gift from beyond the grave. When the dog is brutally killed, the cliché is twisted so it becomes acceptable.

✓ **Think outside the box**. Each story needs a different kind of protagonist. Some stories need positive central characters, others need a negative one. How can you get the audience to relate to any character? By using conflict as a source of interest and identification. Don't forget that sometimes the protagonist is a group of characters sharing the same goal, even if there is a main protagonist within that group. Occasionally, the line is blurred between protagonist and antagonist. This can make the story more interesting as long as it doesn't prevent the audience from getting emotionally involved. This is what stories such as *Heat* or *Prisoners* achieve. These stories might not be for everyone, but they certainly found an audience.

Connected Problems in This Book
- 28 The Protagonist Is Not Strong Enough
- 01 We Don't Care About the Protagonist
- 05 The Characters Are Flat, Two-Dimensional
- 13 The Characters Are Stereotypes or Clichés

Sections in Screenwriting Unchained
- 'Hero vs Protagonist' in 2.3 Craft the Draft
- 3.4 Hands-On: Growth, Change or Steadfast?

Sections in 12 Ways to a Stronger Screenplay
- Set-up / Story World
- Managing Conflict (Who Wants / Needs What and Why?)
- Managing Information (Who Knows What When?)
- Character (Growth, Change or Steadfast?)

38 The Plot Is Contrived

Being told that your plot is contrived may give the impression that your story suffers from some kind of disease. Although it might not make you feel better to say so, this is a common ailment. The good news? It's fully treatable!

First of all, what does this note mean? Simply that there isn't enough causality (cause and effect) in the story. What happens doesn't seem to stem from the characters (who they are, their actions, their decisions) but from the writer forcing these events to happen in order to serve the plot or the theme.

Writing a screenplay is a bit like setting up one of those domino displays, where after hours if not days of preparation, you push the first domino and cause and effect produces a complex, mesmerising pattern. As a writer, you're allowed that first single push, but after that everything should seem to flow organically in the story, without any external intervention.

This means you have to design characters so that what they do throughout the story agrees with what we've learnt about them and what they've done earlier. Situations, events, even steps in the character's evolution should happen as a logical consequence of what has happened previously. You can start a story with a coincidence, you might get away with one more during the course of the story, but ending with one is certainly ill-advised. Of course this doesn't mean that everything should be predictable. That would be immensely boring. You can still have twists and characters behaving in surprising ways, as long as once it's happened, or once the audience has the relevant information, it makes sense.

Solutions

So how do we deal with this note? Here are a few pointers:

✓ **Look at the key events in your story,** except possibly the inciting event (the event that triggers the protagonist's goal), and check that things happen either because of who the characters are (how they have been designed, according to their main characteristics) or because of what happened before in the story. You're looking for causality (cause and effect) in your screenplay. One of the best tools you can use to achieve this is a step-outline: the whole story over a few pages, with a few lines, one paragraph at most for each key step in the story. One step can be a whole dramatic sequence; there is no need for detail in a step-outline. The same can be achieved with index cards or a beat sheet if you're more familiar with these. Once you have this short document, each step (or index card / beat) should feel like a logical consequence of what's come before, and should clearly cause further events in the story. If you are able to take a step out, if you can swap two steps in the outline without disrupting the story, it usually means that there is not enough causality in your story, and that's one of the main reasons you're getting this note. You'll find more about this need for causality in 25 The Narrative Is Episodic or Repetitive.

✓ **If some story events or situations take place only because you need them to happen to serve the plot or the theme,** try to connect them either to one of the characters (which might mean changing the design of the character or the nature of the event), or to a previous event in the story. If that's not possible, find a way to plant this event by foreshadowing either a character trait or a cause earlier in the story that will lead to this event. For example, if you need your protagonist to quit their job in the middle of the story, make sure that you've seeded reasons for them wanting to leave before that, otherwise such a sudden move might feel contrived. Don't have one convenient argument with their boss that leads them to quit when you need them to.

✓ **Look at the dialogue in your screenplay,** and check whether your characters are constantly explaining what they are doing, or why they are doing it. This is often a tell-tale sign. The writer senses that they are pushing the story or the characters in an artificial direction, so they try to justify it using dialogue. You really need to weed out most of the dialogue explaining what the characters think or feel, or why they have done something. In most cases, it shouldn't be necessary. If events are triggered by what the characters have done before, by the decisions they have made earlier in the story, their actions should be self-explanatory. Try to show who the characters are, find the right conflict to reveal some inner truth about them, and you won't need to have them (or other characters) explain their actions.

✓ **Look at the main characters in your screenplay and try to map their evolution.** This means looking at the way they grow or change between the beginning and the end of the film. Usually, you can find four to six main psychological or emotional steps that make this evolution possible and believable. Not all characters need to change, especially if you're not dealing with a character-led story, but most characters will at least grow in some way. When you look at the steps of their evolution, do they make sense? Can you take one step out, or is there a step missing? Maybe two steps need to be swapped for the evolution to be more convincing? This kind of evolution map gives you at character level what a step outline (or index cards / beat sheet) brings at story level. Ensuring that the character evolution is consistent can help you make the plot less contrived. Often, when a problem is spotted in the plot (as is the case when you're given this note), the solution lies in the characters.

✓ **If you're dealing with a theme-led story** (a multi-stranded narrative where many strands explore the same problem usually located in society), you'll have to include more coincidences than usual. This is because you need to find ways to connect strands together, and often that comes through a coincidence: two characters from different strands meet by accident, the same random event impacts characters from different strands, etc. In this case, if you don't want the plot to feel contrived, you have to pump up causality in the rest of the story – through planting and pay-off – in order to override the negative impact of the coincidences. Make sure that as many events as possible have consequences, and that events are mostly rooted in what has happened previously in that strand or another one, or stem naturally from the character design, their actions or their decisions. This is key to developing a **theme-led story**. You need to up your causality gauge before it takes a hit from each coincidence. Otherwise after a couple of coincidences you're running on empty and the plot will feel contrived. For more details on planting and pay-off, see 25 The Narrative Is Episodic or Repetitive and also the list at the end of this chapter.

✓   **Finally, let go of any story theory that tells you that all stories have to follow the same pattern, that there are mandatory steps or plot points in every story.** Having a "Refusal of the Call" or an "All is Lost" moment isn't appropriate for all stories (don't worry if you're not familiar with these terms). Trying to force these steps into a story that doesn't need them might lead to you getting this note, because it will bring a degree of artificiality and predictability to the story, making the plot feel contrived. It can be reassuring, when you start out, to believe that following a well-established paradigm is a key to success, but there are no absolute rules in screenwriting. Mastering flexible tools and principles is a far more interesting way to guide your creativity. The earlier you let go of prescriptive rules, the faster you'll stop seeing this note (and quite a few others). This is discussed in more detail in 19 The Script Feels Formulaic.

Connected Problems in This Book

- 30 The Script Contains Too Much Exposition
- 31 The Drama / Conflict Is Told But Not Shown

Sections in Screenwriting Unchained

- 'Planting and Pay-Off' in 2.1 Behind the Scenes
- 6.2 Story Design Tools

Sections in 12 Ways to a Stronger Screenplay

- Character (Change, Growth or Steadfast?)
- Planting, Pay-Off and Visual Storytelling
- Satisfying Ending

39 The Theme Overshadows the Story

Usually, when the theme overshadows the story, it means that the theme (what the story is about) gets in the way of plot or character development.

There could be all sorts of reasons for this, but let's look at the most common ones.

Sometimes the writer feels so strongly about the theme that they are using every character, every scene to convey the meaning of the story (what they want it to be about) in an overly direct way. We can picture the writer on a soapbox, using characters as a megaphone to try and convert us, rather than designing three-dimensional characters that are trying to solve a problem connected to the theme. This is where the antiquated saying still applies: "If I want to send a message, I use Western Union", although today we should probably say Twitter. No one wants to feel they are being preached to when they're watching a movie.

Other times, it could be that you are developing a **theme-led story**, a multi-stranded narrative with many subplots called strands and no main plot. If you're not familiar with this story-type – which is hard to get right – you may not be handling it properly. The reader / audience may understand that all these storylines are connected to the same theme, but if the strands are not expertly designed and weaved together, the overall story can feel didactic rather than moving or entertaining.

There is nothing wrong with having a strong theme in a story. Most masterpieces, in any genre, tend to have one. In fact, it's very difficult to write a great story about nothing. Developing a theme-led story is fine if that's your intention, but it should be done in such a way that it doesn't detract from efficient character and plot development, which is the tricky part.

Solutions

So how do we deal with this note?

✓ **Are all the characters expressing your own personal point of view about the theme? Are all the scenes hammering this single opinion, leaving little room for the story to develop organically?** It's great that you know what your story is about, but this is not what the audience is primarily interested in. We do appreciate meaningful stories, but only if they deliver emotion and entertainment as well. So you need to look at your theme and think about the best way to express it through a story that primarily explores either a problem connected to a main dramatic action (**plot-led story,** the main problem lies outside of the protagonist) or a main dramatic evolution (**character-led story,** the main problem lies within the protagonist). If the problem lies in society, can't be solved or is spiritual, you might explore it through a set of storylines connected to the same theme (**theme-led story,** see below). That way, you'll develop a main dramatic action or dramatic evolution, or possibly a combination if you go for the theme-led option, but your characters won't come across as puppets used to express your own point of view.

✓ **Make sure that some of the characters in your story represent an opposite point of view.** Whether they are antagonists (characters whose goal is in direct opposition to your protagonist in a **plot-led story**) or catalysts (characters who help the protagonist to change in a **character-led story**), this should make the story more interesting. Drama isn't a statement, it's a struggle. This fight can be internal in a character-led story, or external in a plot-led story, but it's dynamic, not static.

There is usually some evolution caused by the dramatic action, or some action caused by the dramatic evolution. The meaning of the story comes both from this evolution (growth or change of the protagonist, or of the relationships between the characters) and from the outcome (positive or negative, the protagonist succeeds or fails). The theme overshadows the story if you hammer the same meaning repeatedly, instead of designing the narrative so that meaning is conveyed organically by the characters' evolution and the ending.

✓ **Try to make it so that your theme raises a question, and explore this question through the whole story**, as if you had no clear-cut opinion from the get go. You want the audience to reach a conclusion because the story itself has made your point, not because your audience had your beliefs forced on them. So find a way to stage an interesting, dynamic debate, with pros and cons that often change during the story according to what happens or what we learn, rather than a static, didactic "message". Debate here doesn't mean that this exploration should take place through dialogue. It means that your exploration of the question raised takes different angles into consideration. The best way to achieve this is to remain open-minded, play devil's advocate and look at the situation from the point of view of all the characters (including those that represent a point of view opposed to your own).

✓ **Consider developing your story as a multi-stranded narrative (a theme-led story)** if the meaning of the story interests you more than a main dramatic action or evolution – especially if the question, the problem raised by the theme, lies in society, is abstract, spiritual or philosophical, or can't be resolved by the end of the story. If you take this direction, the reader / audience should understand that the theme is the main focus of the story, but you'll also make sure that each storyline delivers a narrative that is moving and entertaining, so that the theme doesn't overshadow the story.

✓ **Ensure that you make a distinction between a theme-led story** (a multi-stranded narrative when the main problem lies in society and all the strands are connected to the same theme) **and an ensemble piece or a plot-led or character-led story with co-protagonists** (a story with a main dramatic action / evolution where the protagonist is a group of characters sharing the same dramatic goal). For example, *Crash, Game of Thrones* and *Dunkirk* are theme-led stories, because there is no clear protagonist, only a collection of strands connected to the same theme, hence they are multi-stranded narratives. But *The Magnificent Seven, Saving Private Ryan* and *Little Miss Sunshine* are not theme-led, because there is a main dramatic action / evolution. In these films, different characters share the same conscious goal or unconscious need so we have multiple characters forming the protagonist rather than a multi-stranded narrative. This is important because a story doesn't need to be theme-led to have a strong theme or convey a strong meaning. Designing your story as a multi-stranded narrative or as an ensemble piece could help you address this note, but they are designed differently because they don't share the same story-type.

Connected Problems in This Book:
* 02 We Don't Care About the Story
* 10 The Ending Doesn't Work
* 25 The Narrative Is Episodic or Repetitive
* 29 The Plot Is Slowed Down By Unconnected Storylines
* 38 The Plot Is Contrived
* 12 The Characters Are Too Similar
* 21 There Is Too Much Dialogue
* 24 There Is No Clear Antagonist

Sections in Screenwriting Unchained:
* 'Theme' in 2.3 Craft the Draft
* 4.0 Developing a Theme-Led Story

Sections in 12 Ways to a Stronger Screenplay:
* Theme (What Is the Story About?)
* Set-Up / Story World
* Satisfying Ending

40 The Premise Is an Artificial Excuse For Action

As you probably know, a premise is the idea or argument on which the story is based. You're likely to get this feedback when your story design focuses on set pieces and action sequences rather than a character (or a group of characters) trying to overcome a problem that audiences can relate to, especially when the situation is caused by an unmotivated antagonist.

The audience is not there just to watch special effects or stunts. They want to experience excitement, emotion and identification. Gripping set pieces and cool special effects will soon turn into an expensive mix of noise and boredom if characters are flaky and if the story has no theme.

Solutions

So how do we address this? Here are a few pointers:

✓ **Look for a theme. What does your story have to say? How does it reflect our experience of life?** It doesn't have to be something profound or philosophical or even challenging, but does the story have meaning? Is it something that a modern audience can connect to, even if the story is set in the distant past or a dystopian future? There are many ways to establish this connection, but the two most common are to find a universal human value that has relevance irrespective of time and place (friendship, protection of family, jealousy, etc) or to transpose an acute problem in modern society (say racism or economic difficulties) and explore it in a different world.

So identify what your story is about, at a thematic level. For example, *Heat* isn't about a series of heists, it's about respect between two enemies and emotional vulnerability.

Then explore this theme throughout your story. It could be through a character-led element tied to the evolution of the protagonist of a plot-led story, such as Ryan's Stone's need to move on from her daughter's death in *Gravity*, which is about rebirth and resilience; or it could be a subplot set around a character who isn't the protagonist of the main plot, but still allows us to explore the theme in a way that is, of course, connected to the main dramatic action. *Mad Max: Fury Road* provides a good example. The love story between Nux and Capable explores the themes of redemption and sacrifice, and is connected to the main plot: Nux's sacrifice is, ultimately, what allows the co-protagonists to reach their goal. It's neither original, nor highly philosophical, but it brings some emotional depth to the story.

✓ **A story might feel artificial because it's not believable.** In your eagerness to get things started (kudos to you!), are you brushing past obvious objections (regarding story logic, coincidences, etc) hoping that no one will notice? It's great to take less than ten to fifteen minutes to start a story, but not if it prevents suspension of disbelief. The audience has expectations and this is a bit like foregoing foreplay: your partner (your audience) is unlikely to be grateful. So if there are things in the set-up that don't make sense, try to address them. Sometimes it's as easy as having a character ask the question that's on everyone's mind, and finding an answer convincing enough to put it behind us. You're allowed one coincidence to start a story, no more. So if you need more than one, you might want to re-think your set-up.

✓ **Look at the antagonist's motivation.** There isn't an antagonist in every story. However, most **plot-led stories** (where the main problem lies outside the protagonist) have one. It's a natural tendency to look at the story from the point of view of the protagonist, but that can leave plot holes. An antagonist who has no clear reason to oppose the protagonist can make the whole premise seem contrived and unbelievable. Beyond motivation, an antagonist should also be resourceful, original and persistent. So try to look at the story from the point of view of the antagonist. Ask yourself what the antagonist's goal is, why they are so determined to reach it and, in doing so, how they cause conflict for the protagonist. It could be very primal if it's a character we can't reason with, such as the antagonist in *Jaws*, *Alien* or *The Terminator*. But otherwise, keep in mind that every single antagonist is the protagonist of their own story. Only cardboard villains see themselves as the baddy, and enjoy it. You don't need to go as far as giving the antagonist the goal of saving the world as in *Inferno* or *Avengers: Infinity War*, but it will usually help to come up with a good reason for the antagonist to oppose the protagonist. Tackling any weakness in this area should help make the story less artificial and more believable.

✓ **Look at the protagonist's evolution.** Just because your story is **plot-led** doesn't mean that there is no room for your central character to evolve. Protagonists don't need to change if there is nothing wrong with them, but they often need to grow. This growth can either be what they need to learn, to improve on in order to be able to reach their goal, or it can be the way they evolve as a result of the intense conflict they have experienced. Giving your protagonist some room to grow, often through a character-led subplot, will help you give them – and the story – more depth. Just try to avoid the obvious clichés (estranged partners, dead child, etc) because you risk making the story feel too familiar, especially if these characters are not connected to a strong theme.

✓ **Can you make the protagonist partially responsible for what happens to them in the story?** This could diminish any melodramatic aspect of the story that might have triggered this note. We have a melodrama when a succession of external obstacles fall upon an innocent protagonist. Action / adventure films are the modern equivalent of melodramas. Along with finding a theme and giving some depth to the characters, giving the protagonist some responsibility in what happens might help. It could be something that the protagonist does (or doesn't do) at the beginning, or something in their personality that causes the story to happen to them rather than anyone else. If you link this characterisation element to a character-led subplot, you could hit two birds with one stone. For example, in *Misery*, Paul Sheldon wants to write more serious books and kills the protagonist of his commercially successful series, Misery. This not only plays a part in his ordeal (Nurse Annie goes ballistic when she finds out that he's killed her favourite character), it also feeds his evolution as a writer.

✓   **What's at stake in the story?** Often this will make the difference between an action-led narrative and a story with more emotional depth. For example, is your protagonist just doing their job? If they are a cop, a journalist investigating a case or a special agent on a mission, can you find ways to make it personal so that what's at stake is something that we all care about? The convention, in these films, is that even if the protagonist risks their lives, we assume that they can't die. So instead of giving them the goal of "doing their job", we can, for example, put the life of someone they care about (partner, child, parent, pet) at stake. Consider raising the stakes by making it so that it's not just about "saving the world". It makes it more personal and it can introduce a dilemma (do I save the world or the people I love?). *Mission Impossible: Fallout* does this effectively. Of course, this can be a cliché if done in a non-inventive way, but it became a cliché for a reason: if the genre means you can't kill your protagonist without killing your story, or even worse, your sequel, then how do you rack up the conflict? You can either give them internal obstacles, such as the fear of water for Chief Brody in *Jaws*, or make it personal and find a way to hit them where it hurts: emotionally rather than physically. More on this in <u>02 We Don't Care About the Story</u>.

Connected Problems in This Book

*   20 The Conflict Is Artificial or Inconsequential
*   19 The Script Feels Formulaic

- 06 The Character Logic Is Fuzzy
- 02 We Don't Care About the Story
- 01 We Don't Care About the Protagonist
- 05 The Characters Are Flat, Two-Dimensional
- 13 The Characters Are Stereotypes or Clichés
- 26 The Villains or Antagonists Are Weak or Unconvincing
- 28 The Protagonist Is Not Strong Enough
- 37 The Protagonist Is a Conventional Hero

Sections in Screenwriting Unchained

- 1.1 Is Maslow Running the Show?
- 2.3 Craft the Draft
- '*Gravity*' in 2.5 Case Studies

Sections in 12 Ways to a Stronger Screenplay

- Story-Type and Genre
- M-Factor (What's at Stake?)
- Theme (What is the Story About?)
- Set-Up / Story World
- Character (Growth, Change or Steadfast?)

Conclusion

As this book isn't meant to be read from cover to cover, there shouldn't be a conclusion really, but I thought I'd write one for those of you who have valiantly ploughed through the whole thing.

I hope that I've succeeded in explaining the most common problems in a screenplay, translating vague symptoms or cryptic notes into underlying problems and actionable advice. Ideally, this led you to a clear path towards resolving some of these issues, should they be present in your story.

I also tried to bust a few myths in the process, such as "the protagonist is the character who changes the most in a story" or "if the audience doesn't care about your protagonists, make them more likeable".

Of course there is always more than one way to skin (or rather save) a cat, so I hope that I strike the right balance between providing advice specific enough to be helpful, and reminding the reader that keeping an open mind for exceptions is key when working in script development.

There are often different causes for the same symptom, so there can't be a simple, unique way of addressing each problem. It's difficult to help a writer resolve creative issues in an original piece of work that you haven't read without spelling out arbitrary or generic rules, but that's nevertheless what I've tried to achieve.

I'd love to hear from you if some of these sections have helped with some of your stories or if you think I've missed a common problem you'd like to see addressed in any future edition. Please look at the last section, If You Want to Find Out More... to get in touch and let us know.

In the meantime, I wish you the best with all of your projects. Screenwriting is incredibly hard work, but it can be immensely rewarding. I hope this book leaves you inspired and energised for your next draft and that you can't wait to get started.

As Dory says in *Finding Nemo*, "Just keep swimming..."

Story-Type Method Glossary

Note: When a definition references another **term** from this glossary, it will appear in *italics* the first time it's mentioned in the definition. When a definition references other chapters from this book, these links are <u>underlined</u>. Most of the terms and concepts related to the Story-Type Method are defined and introduced along with the method itself in the first volume in the series, '*Screenwriting Unchained*' as well as in the Advanced Development online course. See 'If You Want to Find Out More' at the end of this book for more details.

A

Act: Main division in a screenplay. This division can be logistical, which means based on an arbitrary number of pages / minutes (30-60-30 Three-Act paradigm or its 25-25-25-25 Four-Act variant with a *midpoint*) in a feature screenplay or the number of commercial breaks in a TV episode / TV movie (leading to two, four, five or seven acts). These *logistical acts* only apply to the whole screenplay. They are about format rather than structure. See *Three-Act Structure (logistical)*. Act divisions can also follow a more flexible dramatic structure, for example before, during and after a main *dramatic action* or *evolution*. These *dramatic acts* have no predetermined length and apply not only to the whole story, but also to its parts: *dramatic sequences, scenes, subplots* or *strands*, thanks to the *fractal aspect of story structure*. See *Three-Act Structure (dramatic)*, <u>03 The Story Takes Too Long to Start</u>, <u>19 The Script Feels Formulaic</u> and <u>35 The Script Is Unnecessarily Complex</u>.

Action: See *Dramatic Action*.

Antagonist: *Character* (or group of characters sharing the same *goal*) whose objective is in direct opposition to the protagonist's goal, hence constitutes the main source of conflict for the *protagonist*. Not all stories need an antagonist. In *character-led* stories, where the main problem lies within the protagonist, the protagonist *is* the antagonist, and we have instead a *catalyst character*. An antagonist isn't the same as a *villain*. See 18 There Is No Clear Protagonist, 24 There Is No Clear Antagonist and 26 The Villains or Antagonists Are Weak or Unconvincing.

Anti-Climax: Disappointing or predictable *ending* (usually of a story, but it could be of a *dramatic sequence* or even a *scene*), often due to a lack of *conflict* or because of a *deus ex machina*. See 22 The Ending Is an Anti-Climax, 23 The Ending Is a *Deus Ex Machina* and 10 The Ending Doesn't Work.

B

Backstory: See *Character Backstory*.

Beginning: According to the logistical *Three-Act Structure* paradigm, the first twenty-five to thirty minutes of a two-hour screenplay. In the *Story-Type Method*, it's the first ten to fifteen minutes of the film, also called the *set-up*. One of the most important parts of a story, along with the *ending*. It usually introduces the characters and the *story world*, and sets up a main *dramatic action* (plot-led story), *evolution* (character-led story) or *theme* (theme-led story). Ideally, it gives an indication of *what's at stake* in the story. See 03 The Story Takes Too Long to Start, 02 We Don't Care About the Story and 19 The Script Feels Formulaic.

C

Catalyst Character: *Character* who pushes / helps the *protagonist* to change in a *character-led* story (or in the *character-led subplot* of a *plot-led story*). Often looks like an antagonistic character because they tend to oppose the protagonist's *conscious goal*. In fact, catalyst characters are *co-protagonists* on the protagonist's *unconscious need* to change. Examples: Maeve in '*Sex Education*'. Tiffany in '*Silver Linings Playbook*', Driss in '*The Intouchables*', Jonathan "The Duke" Mardukas in '*Midnight Run*'. See 01 We Don't Care About the Protagonist, 05 The Characters Are Flat, Two-Dimensional, 16 The Scenes Are Aimless, There Is No Dramatic Conflict, 19 The Script Feels Formulaic and 24 There Is No Clear Antagonist.

Causality: Cause and effect. When events happen in a story as a result of what has happened before, and when they also cause further events in a story, there is causality. When events happen due to chance, luck or coincidence, and when they have few consequences later, there isn't enough causality. To check for causality in a story, write a step outline (the whole story over a few pages with one paragraph per step) and see if you can take out or swap some of these steps without disrupting the whole story. If this is possible, get rid of these steps or find a way to connect them with what has happened previously and what happens next. Pay extra attention to *subplots* and verify that they are sufficiently connected to the *main plot*. See 25 The Narrative Is Episodic or Repetitive and 38 The Plot Is Contrived.

Character: The central element of story, along with *plot* (what happens in the story) and *theme* (what the story is about). Story *is* character. If we don't care about the characters, we won't care about the story. See 01 We Don't Care About the Protagonist, 02 We Don't Care About the Story, 05 The Characters Are Flat, Two-Dimensional, 06 The Character Logic Is Fuzzy, 12 The Characters Are Too Similar and 13 The Characters Are Stereotypes or Clichés.

Character Backstory: What happened to the *character* before the story started. Writers need to work on the characters' backstories to be able to write about them, but the audience doesn't need to be told all this information. This is why it's called backstory. Most of it should remain in the background and there's no need to bring it to the front, except the part that, if unknown, could prevent an emotional identification. See 14 The Characters' Backstories Are Irrelevant / Pointless.

Character Change: When a *character* follows the wrong path, they need to change. This often means that they have to move on from a traumatic event in their past that is holding them up, or to become aware of an internal flaw and correct it. The audience will only want a character to change if they believe that there is hope they might do so, and if the character isn't happy (consciously or not) with the way they are. Usually a character change is associated with the protagonist's *evolution* in a *character-led story*. See *Character Growth*, *Steadfast Character*, and 05 The Characters Are Flat, Two-Dimensional.

Character Growth: When a character follows the right path, they don't need to change because there is nothing wrong with them or with what they're trying to achieve. However, they might need to grow (get stronger, resolve a minor internal issue, face an internal fear) in order to stand a chance of reaching their *goal*. Alternatively, they might grow as a consequence of the conflict they have experienced while trying to reach their goal. A character growth is often associated with the protagonist's *evolution* in a *plot-led story*. See *Character Change, Steadfast Character*, and 05 The Characters Are Flat, Two-Dimensional.

Character Evolution (or **Character Arc**): When a character is different at the end of the story, they have evolved. This evolution can be a change or a growth (see above). Usually, the *protagonist* of a *character-led story* changes (or fails to change if it's a tragic ending) while the protagonist of a *plot-led story* grows (or remains steadfast). Not all characters need to evolve. A character who doesn't evolve is called a *steadfast character*. See *Character Change, Character Growth* and 05 The Characters Are Flat, Two-Dimensional.

Character Inciting Event: Event that triggers the unconscious need to change in a character. See *Inciting Event (or Inciting Incident)* and 03 The Story Takes Too Long to Start.

Character-Led Story: A story where the main problem lies within the *protagonist*. In such a story, the protagonist *is* the *antagonist*: Most of the *conflict* comes from within the protagonist. What's primarily at stake is whether the protagonist will change or not, whether they'll find a way of overcoming their inner flaw. The backbone of the story is the *main dramatic evolution* of the protagonist. Because we resist change, we need conflict to force the character to evolve. Usually, this conflict comes from a *catalyst*, a character who pushes / helps the protagonist to change. In a character-led story, the protagonist is the character who changes the most, but that's not necessarily true for other story-types. See 18 There Is No Clear Protagonist.

Character-led subplot: See *Subplot*.

Cliffhanger: An unresolved *conflict* at the end of a *scene* or a *sequence* in a script, an episode or a season in a TV series or before we leave a *strand* in a *multi-stranded narrative*. This is usually achieved by leaving the protagonist in a difficult situation, or by dropping an information-bomb (*surprise*, set-up or resolution of a *dramatic irony*, resolution of a *mystery*) that leaves the audience wanting to know what's going to happen next. See 04 The Story Is Linear, Feels Predictable and 34 Too Many Questions Are Left Unanswered.

Climax: The moment, scene or sequence towards the end of a story during which you provide an answer to the *dramatic question*. As soon as we understand who wants or needs what and why in a story, we enter *dramatic Act 2* and start wondering "Will the protagonist reach their *goal*?" This is the dramatic question. The climax, usually the most conflictual moment in the story, brings an answer to this question and marks the end of the main *dramatic action* or *evolution* that shaped the story if it was *plot-led* or *character-led*. We enter *dramatic Act 3* in a story after the climax. Thanks to the *fractal aspect of story structure*, we can also find a climax at the end of a *dramatic scene*, *sequence*, *subplot* or *strand* if they are designed using a *dramatic Three-Act Structure*. See 10 The Ending Doesn't Work, 22 The Ending Is an Anti-Climax and 23 The Ending Is a *Deus Ex Machina*.

Co-protagonists: When two or more *characters* share the same *conscious goal* or *unconscious need*, they are co-protagonists if this group of characters experience the most conflict in the story. For example, in *'Saving Private Ryan'*, all the soldiers led by Captain Miller have the same *goal*, stated in the title. In *'Little Miss Sunshine'*, all the family members have both the same conscious goal (to get Olive to the pageant in time) and the same unconscious need (to become less dysfunctional). In *'Stranger Things'*, Will's mother, brother and friends — joined by Hopper — have the same goal, which is to find Will and rescue him. In *'The Walking Dead'*, Rick Grimes is the first and main protagonist, but all the survivors that are part of his constantly evolving group are co-protagonists as they share the same goal: staying alive while protecting each other. See *protagonist* and 18 There Is No Clear Protagonist.

Conflict: One of the main elements of drama, mostly used to generate realism, interest, *identification*, *emotion* and cause an *evolution*. A conflict can be serious or humorous (most gags are conflicts). Conflict can be used to disguise *foreshadowing* or to make *exposition* more palatable. It usually comes from the opposition between a *goal* and *obstacles*, whether they are external or internal. Conflict can also be generated through *managing information*, for

---

example using *dramatic irony*. See <u>20 The Conflict Is Artificial or Inconsequential</u>, <u>04 The Story Is Linear, Feels Predictable</u> and <u>16 The Scenes Are Aimless, There Is No Dramatic Conflict</u>.

Cold Start: When a story starts with a *protagonist* who doesn't know where they are and doesn't remember their past due to some condition (usually amnesia), we have a cold start. This sets up a *mystery* about the protagonist's past, but because we know as much as the protagonist, it doesn't prevent emotional *identification*. On the contrary, we team up with the protagonist to resolve this mystery. A cold start often leads to flashbacks gradually revealing the missing information about the protagonist's past, as they start to remember. Examples: *'The Walking Dead'*, *'The Bourne Identity'*, *'Predators'*, *'Before I Go to Sleep'*, *'The Maze Runner'*, *'Cowboys & Aliens'*. See <u>03 The Story Takes Too Long to Start</u> and <u>01 We Don't Care About the Protagonist</u>.

Conceptual Identification: See *Identification*.

Conscious Goal: What a character consciously wants, what they are trying to achieve actively. This isn't necessarily the same as their *unconscious need*. The protagonist's conscious goal defines the *main dramatic action* in a *plot-led story*. See <u>05 The Characters Are Flat, Two-Dimensional</u>.

Contrived: When events happen in a story only to serve the plot or the theme, rather than stemming from the characters and what has happened to them previously, we say that <u>38 The Plot Is Contrived</u>.

D

Deus Ex Machina: An unplanted element that helps the *protagonist* to get out of trouble at the end of a story, a *dramatic sequence*, or a *dramatic scene*. Initially, the expression comes from ancient plays, where the plot was resolved by gods being lowered onto stage on a mechanical platform: "Deus ex machina" – a god from a machine. See <u>23 The Ending Is a *Deus Ex Machina*</u>.

Dialogue: What the characters say. Good dialogue is an important asset in any screenplay; poor dialogue can easily put the reader off. However, from a design point of view, it's the least important part. See <u>15 The Dialogue Is Cheesy, Full of Action Movie Clichés</u> and <u>21 There Is Too Much Dialogue</u>.

Dogmatic: See *Formula, Formulaic*.

Dramatic Act: See *Three-Act Structure (dramatic)*.

Dramatic Three-Act Structure: See *Three-Act Structure (dramatic)*.

Dramatic Action: Action defined by what the *protagonist* consciously wants. In a *plot-led story*, the protagonist's *goal* usually remains the same over the entirety of *dramatic Act 2*, so we have a main dramatic action that shapes the whole story. This main dramatic action is often cut down into more manageable units called *dramatic sequences*, which are a succession of scenes connected to the same *subgoal* (way to reach the goal). See 02 We Don't Care About the Story, 07 The Story Sags in the Middle.

Dramatic Evolution: An evolution defined by the *protagonist's* unconscious need to change or grow. In a *character-led story*, the protagonist's need to change usually remains the same over the entirety of *dramatic Act 2*, so we have a main dramatic evolution that shapes the whole story. This main dramatic evolution is often cut down into more manageable units called *dramatic sequences*, which are a succession of scenes connected to the same *subgoal* (what the protagonist consciously wants in the sequence). These sequences provide ways for the protagonist to experience the *conflict* that is going to force them to change, one step at a time. A dramatic evolution, usually connected to the protagonist's need to grow, can also shape a character-led *subplot* in a *plot-led story*. See *character change* and 05 The Characters Are Flat, Two-Dimensional.

Dramatic Irony: When the audience knows something that at least one character on screen is unaware of. This can be used to generate *suspense* in a thriller (Hitchcock's "bomb under the table"), humour in a comedy (most of the characters in '*Tootsie*' are unaware that Dorothy Michaels isn't a woman), and tension in drama (the characters at the beginning of '*Stranger Things*' don't know that there is a Demogorgon on the run and that it has taken Will Byers). A character kept in the dark is the victim of a dramatic irony. It works in three steps: 1) Set-up, when you give the audience the information, 2) Exploitation, when you make the most of the conflict (humour, drama) generated by the dramatic irony and 3) Resolution, when the victim finds out. Dramatic irony is one of the most powerful tools in the writer's toolbox and is linked to managing information, along with *mystery*, *surprise* and *suspense*. See 04 The Story Is Linear, Feels Predictable and 19 The Script Feels Formulaic.

Dramatic Question: The main hook that keeps the audience interested during *dramatic Act 2*. In a *plot-led story*, it's "Will the protagonist get what they want?" In a *character-led story*, it's "Will the protagonist get what they need?" This applies to the whole story but also to its parts when there is something clearly at stake in each dramatic unit (strand, act, storyline, dramatic sequence or scene). See 02 We Don't Care About the Story, 04 The Story Is Linear, Feels Predictable and 16 The Scenes Are Aimless, There Is No Dramatic Conflict.

Dramatic Scene: A scene where something is clearly at stake, i.e. we understand who wants what and why in the scene and what stands in the way. A new dramatic scene starts when the *protagonist* or the *goal* changes. A new logistical scene starts when the location or the time changes. As a result, a dramatic scene can be made up of many logistical scenes. For example, a single dramatic scene can start in the kitchen, continue in the bathroom and end in the bedroom. This would be three different logistical scenes, but a single dramatic scene if the protagonist and the goal remain the same over the three logistical scenes. See 16 The Scenes Are Aimless, There Is No Dramatic Conflict.

Dramatic Sequence: A succession of *dramatic scenes* where the *protagonist's goal* in each scene is connected to the same *subgoal*, either as a way of reaching it, or as a way of dealing with the consequences of having reached it (or having failed to reach it). A dramatic sequence can also be designed around a *dramatic irony*, in which case an *ironic question* (How and when will the victim find out, and how will they react?) replaces or supplements the *dramatic question* (Will the protagonist of the sequence reach the subgoal?). The protagonist of a dramatic sequence is usually the story protagonist, but occasionally it can be a different character, especially in a *multi-stranded narrative* or TV Series. There is no set number of dramatic sequences in each act, and there is no set duration for each dramatic sequence. A dramatic sequence can be as short as a few minutes, and as long as sixty minutes or more. See 07 The Story Sags in the Middle.

Dramatic Structure: See *Three-Act Structure (dramatic)*.

E

Emotion: What we want to deliver through storytelling, along with entertainment and meaning. Emotion is usually generated using *conflict*. The most moving moments in a story (for example the ending) tend to *pay off* what has happened before in the story, and are often delivered using *visual storytelling*. See 27 The Script Is Cold, Unemotional, 35 The Script Is Unnecessarily Complex and 10 The Ending Doesn't Work.

Emotional Identification: See *Identification*.

Encore Twist: A surprise at the beginning of *dramatic Act 3* that re-launches the same *dramatic action* for the protagonist, when we thought the action was over because it looked like the protagonist had succeeded, or had failed and given up. See 10 The Ending Doesn't Work, 17 The Script Loses the Plot in the Third Act.

Ending: What you leave the audience with, so one of the most important parts of a story, along with the *beginning* (also called the *set-up*). We can enjoy both happy and unhappy endings. What's key is whether the ending is satisfying or not, as most of the meaning of the story is conveyed through its ending. A satisfying ending is key to getting positive word-of-mouth. An unsatisfying ending can ruin an otherwise good story. See 10 The Ending Doesn't Work, 17 The Script Loses the Plot in the Third Act, and 34 Too Many Questions Are Left Unanswered.

Episodic: A story is episodic when it feels like a succession of disconnected episodes that could be easily removed or swapped without changing much in the story or its meaning. Poorly designed biopics often suffer from this when they try to tell the whole life of the main character instead of focusing on a main event or finding a different protagonist. Repetition in a story isn't necessarily an issue, it can even be rewarding. For example, in *'Russian Doll'*, *'Groundhog Day'*, *'Edge of Tomorrow'* or *'Source Code'*, the story repeats itself but this is part of a *high-concept* based on *dramatic irony* and *foreshadowing*. Each repetition adds something to the narrative, hence the story isn't seen as episodic. See 25 The Narrative Is Episodic or Repetitive.

Evolution: See *Dramatic Evolution*.

Exception or Hybrid: When a story isn't *plot-led* (the main problem lies outside of the *protagonist*), *character-led* (the main problem lies within the protagonist) or *theme-led* (the main problem lies in society), it might be an exception or a hybrid. Exceptions often have no main problem, or have more than one. They can also be designed using *dramatic irony* ('*Fleabag*', '*The Departed*', '*The Court Jester*', '*The Hand That Rocks the Cradle*'), or with a non-linear or multi-stranded aspect ('*The Secret in Their Eyes*', '*Citizen Kane*', '*L.A. Confidential*', the first season of '*True Detective*'). A hybrid uses more than one story-type over the story. For example, '*Edge of Tomorrow*' starts as character-led (a coward needs to grow a backbone), then becomes a plot-led story (a former coward trying to save the world). '*Breaking Bad*' starts as plot-led (a dying man trying to protect his family), then gradually becomes character-led (a criminal needs to realise he's destroying the very thing he set out to protect: his family). See 18 There Is No Clear Protagonist and 19 The Script Feels Formulaic.

Exploitation: See *Dramatic Irony*.

Exposition: Telling the audience what happened before the story started, or what has happened between scenes. It can be useful and even necessary, but it's the literary part of drama and when there is too much of it or when it's not handled properly, the audience gets bored. See 30 The Script Contains Too Much Exposition.

F

First Act: See *Three-Act Structure (dramatic)*, *Three-Act Structure (logistical)* and 03 The Story Takes Too Long to Start.

Foreshadowing: see *Planting*.

Formula, Formulaic: Any attempt at convincing creators that all stories should follow the same structure or paradigm in a prescriptive, dogmatic way. Usually based on a mandatory number of *logistical acts* or *sequences* of fixed duration, along with steps or plot points supposed to happen in every story at a specific page number: three-act, four-act, five-act, seven-act, eight sequences, fifteen beats, twenty-two steps, etc. The primary consequence of any formula or paradigm is that it reduces the writer's creative freedom and makes the story predictable – hence boring – for the audience. It's fine to use any paradigm that helps with the writing from a productivity point of view, but formulas are about format: they should not be mistaken for structure. See 19 The Script Feels Formulaic, 03 The Story Takes Too Long to Start, 17 The Script Loses the Plot in the Third Act, 38 The Plot Is Contrived, 10 The Ending Doesn't Work.

Fractal Aspect of Story Structure: A property of dramatic structure that means we can design both the whole story and its parts in the same way: if we use a *dramatic structure* to design the whole story around a main *dramatic action* or *evolution*, we define three *dramatic acts* (before, during and after a main dramatic action or evolution). We can use this same tool to design *dramatic acts*, *sequences, scenes, subplots* or *strands*. This is a key aspect of the *Story-Type Method*. See the introduction of *Screenwriting Unchained* and 07 The Story Sags in the Middle as well as 19 The Script Feels Formulaic.

G

Goal: What a character wants (conscious goal) in a story. Same as Objective. What the protagonist wants over the whole story is the main goal. See *Subgoal* and 01 We Don't Care About the Protagonist.

H

Hero: A conceptually positive character who fights – and is often ready to sacrifice themselves – for the greater good. A hero isn't the same a *protagonist*, as the latter doesn't need to be conceptually positive, they only need to experience more conflict than the other characters in the story. See 37 The Protagonist Is a Conventional Hero and 26 The Villains or Antagonists Are Weak or Unconvincing.

Hierarchy of Needs: See *Maslow's Hierarchy of Needs*.

High-Concept: When a story has a striking and easily communicable plot, it's high-concept. Executives and producers love high-concept projects because they are easy to pitch, both to potential partners and to the audience. A high-concept story summarised in a few lines can make someone want to read the script or watch the film / TV series. High-concept stories are often

designed around *dramatic irony* (the audience knows something that at least one character isn't aware of). For example, an out-of-work actor pretends to be an actress in order to get a part and discovers what being a woman really means (*'Tootsie'*). An emotionally wounded woman shares her most intimate self-loathing feelings and thoughts with the audience, except the reason why she's broken, and the result is both moving and funny (first season of *'Fleabag'*). See 35 The Script Is Unnecessarily Complex.
Hybrid: See *Exception*.

I

Inciting Action: Sometimes in a story, we don't have an *inciting event* (see below) but an inciting action: a succession of events in the first *dramatic act* that trigger the *goal* of the *protagonist*. For example, in *'Misery'*, the car accident isn't an inciting event in itself because it only triggers the main situation: Writer Paul Sheldon being looked after by Nurse Annie. Paul also needs to realise that Annie is a nutter before his goal to escape and survive is triggered. We understand this before him, and this *dramatic irony* (we know that Annie is a nutter, he doesn't) shapes some of what would otherwise be a long first *dramatic act*, as we give him the unconscious goal of realising that he's in more trouble than he thinks. See 03 The Story Takes Too Long to Start.

Inciting Event (or Inciting Incident): The event in a story that triggers the protagonist's *goal*. There is not always an inciting event in a story. Sometimes, the protagonist is already trying to reach their goal when the story starts. In *character-led* stories (where the main problem lies within the protagonist), you can look for two inciting events: the *plot* inciting event, that triggers the *conscious goal* of the protagonist, and the *character* inciting event, that triggers their *unconscious need* to change. You can have either, both or none in such stories, but it's interesting to know what to look for. See 03 The Story Takes Too Long to Start.

Identification: In a story, we're after emotional identification, the ability for the audience to feel empathy, to root for one or more *protagonists*. This is not the same as conceptual identification, feeling sympathy, which means that we like the characters or approve of what they are doing. See 01 We Don't Care About the

Protagonist, 02 We Don't Care About the Story and 18 There Is No Clear Protagonist.

Ironic Question: When a *dramatic irony* is set up in the story (the audience knows something that at least one character, the victim, isn't aware of), the audience wonders: How and when will the victim find out, and how will they react? This ironic question is answered when the irony is resolved. When there is a strong dramatic irony that's exploited over most of the story, it can be more important than the *dramatic question* (Who wants / needs what and why?). For example, in *'Tootsie'*, the ironic question is part of the climax of the film, as we want to know how the victims will react when they find out that Dorothy Michaels is a man, not a woman. See 10 The Ending Doesn't Work.

L

Logistical Acts: See *Three-Act Structure (logistical)*.
Logistical Scene: See *Dramatic Scene*.
Logistical Three-Act Structure: See *Three-Act Structure (logistical)*.

M

Main Character: The most important *character*, the character whose life story we're telling, the most fascinating character in a story. Not necessarily the same as *protagonist*. We tell the story of the main character, and we identify emotionally with the protagonist. The protagonist is often the main character as well, but not always. For example, in the first season of *'Stranger Things'*, the protagonist is the group of characters looking for Will Byers, while the main character (and occasional co-protagonist) is Eleven. In many horror or monster movies, we identify with the protagonist, but the antagonist is the main character, the most fascinating character in the story: Nurse Annie in *'Misery'*, the alien in *'Alien'*, the shark in *'Jaws'*. This is why the antagonist is often referenced in the title of such films. In *'Amadeus'*, Mozart is the antagonist and main character but Salieri is the protagonist. See 28 The Protagonist Is Not Strong Enough, 01 We Don't Care About the Protagonist and 18 There Is No Clear Protagonist.

Main Dramatic Action: See *Dramatic Action*.

Main Dramatic Evolution: See *Dramatic Evolution*.

Managing Conflict: An essential part of *story structure* related to defining *who wants or needs what and why* in the story. The main tool used for managing conflict is what we call the basic chain of drama (protagonist, goal, obstacles, conflict, emotion): a *character* trying to reach a *conscious goal* or an *unconscious need*, meeting *obstacles*, which generates *conflict* and *emotion*. See 20 The Conflict Is Artificial or Inconsequential.

Managing Information: An essential part of story structure related to defining *who knows what when* in the story. The main tools used for managing information are *mystery, surprise, dramatic irony* and *suspense*. See 04 The Story Is Linear, Feels Predictable.

Maslow's Hierarchy of Needs: A theory of human psychology defined by Abraham Maslow in 1943. It establishes five levels of human needs, from the most basic (physiology), shared by all human beings, to the most sophisticated (self-actualisation). In between, we find safety, love / belonging and esteem. Maslow proposes that lower levels need to be fulfilled before higher levels can be reached. This has many direct applications to screenwriting regarding audience, genre, story-type, identification and getting the film made. This is detailed in *'Is Maslow Running the Show?'* in the first chapter of *'Screenwriting Unchained'*, the first volume in the *Story-Type Method* series.

Maslow Factor (or M-Factor): An indicator used in the Story-Type Method to estimate the market appeal of a feature or TV Series project / produced work. It's obtained by looking at the target audience, genre and story-type in relation to *Maslow's Hierarchy of Needs*, as well as the budget. The more those elements fit together, the higher the M-Factor. The more there is an inconsistency, the lower. The scale goes from 1 to 5 and it's always a subjective approximation, not an exact value. Still, a low M-Factor can help to identify issues that need to be addressed in order to increase the market appeal of a project and the chances of seeing it commissioned / produced.

Mid-Act Climax: In some stories, it's not possible to have the same *goal* for the *protagonist* over the entirety of *dramatic Act 2*. In that case, we can shape the first half of *dramatic Act 2* over a first goal, give an answer to the first *dramatic question* during a mid-act climax, then have the protagonist pursue another goal – logically connected to the first – during the second half of the story. This second *dramatic action* will be resolved towards the end of dramatic Act 2, in the *climax* of the story. For example, heist movies are often designed with a mid-act climax. The first half of the story is shaped around the preparation of the heist; the heist itself is a mid-act climax (success / failure of the operation); then a second half of the story deals with the logical consequences of the first half: escaping from the police, fighting over the loot, etc. There is a mid-act climax in '*Life is Beautiful*' and in the second season of '*The Walking Dead*'. A mid-act climax isn't the same as a *midpoint*. See 07 The Story Sags in the Middle.

Midpoint: Some say that every story should have a midpoint in the middle of a script, so around minute sixty in a two-hour film. This mandatory plot point is used in the *logistical Three-Act Structure*, but this is about format, not structure. In a good screenplay, something important happens every few minutes, so if you look for a midpoint, you'll find one, but it's unlikely to be significant from a structural point of view. The midpoint can be safely ignored if you find it confusing. Instead, consider using an optional *mid-act climax*, which is a more useful tool. See 07 The Story Sags in the Middle.

Multi-Stranded Narrative: A story that doesn't have a main plot because it has no main *dramatic action* or *dramatic evolution*, but only *subplots* called *strands* connected to the same *theme*. See *Theme-Led Story* as well as 19 The Script Feels Formulaic, 18 There Is No Clear Protagonist and 39 The Theme Overshadows the Story.

Mystery: A mystery is set up when the audience is given enough information to understand that there is something they don't know, but not enough to know what it is. It can provide a good hook to start a story, as the audience will want to find the answer, out of intellectual curiosity. However, it can be off-putting if it lasts too long and can even work against the emotional involvement of the audience, unless other tools linked to *managing information* are used as well: *surprise, dramatic irony* and *suspense*. The worst kind of mystery is when the *protagonist* knows more than the audience over a long period of time about information that is needed in order to understand their actions, decisions or emotions, for example some elements of their *backstory*. This makes an emotional *identification* with such a protagonist difficult if not impossible. See 04 The Story Is Linear, Feels Predictable, 27 The Script Is Cold, Unemotional, 03

The Story Takes Too Long to Start, 08 The Story Is Confusing, 11 The Screenplay Is Written Like a Novel, 10 The Ending Doesn't Work, 17 The Script Loses the Plot in the Third Act, 22 The Ending Is an Anti-Climax, 30 The Script Contains Too Much Exposition, 34 Too Many Questions Are Left Unanswered and 35 The Script Is Unnecessarily Complex.

N

Narrative: The form chosen to convey the *plot* in a story. See 25 The Narrative Is Episodic or Repetitive.

O

Objective: See *Goal*.

Obstacle: Something that stands in the way of a protagonist's *goal* in order to generate conflict. Obstacles can be internal (from the *protagonist*), external (from other characters or nature) or external with an internal origin (from other characters but triggered by the protagonist's actions, decisions or evolution). See 01 We Don't Care About the Protagonist, 20 The Conflict Is Artificial or Inconsequential, 24 There Is No Clear Antagonist and 31 The Drama / Conflict Is Told But Not Shown.

P

Paradigm: See *Formula, Formulaic*.

Pay-Off: See *Planting* below.

Planting (or **foreshadowing**): Introducing an element in a story (object, *character*, *dialogue*, song) so that the audience either accepts it or understands its meaning later in the story, when that element pays off. Useful in order to add *causality* to the story, facilitate *visual storytelling* or avoid a *deus ex machina*. Planting can also be used to generate emotion. See 25 The Narrative Is Episodic or Repetitive, 31 The Drama / Conflict Is Told But Not Shown, 23 The Ending Is a *Deus Ex Machina*.

Plot: The sequence of connected events (not necessarily in chronological order) that happen in a story. One of the main components of story structure, along with *character* and *theme*. Not exactly the same as *Narrative*. See 17 The Script Loses the Plot in the Third Act, 25 The Narrative Is Episodic or Repetitive, 29 The Plot Is Slowed Down By Unconnected Storylines, 38 The Plot Is Contrived.

Plot Inciting Event: See *Inciting Event (or Inciting Incident)*.

Plot-Led Story: A story where the main problem lies outside the protagonist – in other characters or nature. See 18 There Is No Clear Protagonist.

Premise: Idea or argument on which the story is based. See 40 The Premise Is an Artificial Excuse For Action.

Protagonist: The *character* who experiences the most *conflict* in the story, hence the character with whom we identify the most at an emotional level. The word comes from the Greek *protagonistes*, which means "the one who fights in the first row". A helpful image. The protagonist can be a group of characters – called *co-protagonists* – if they share the same goal (*conscious want* or *unconscious need*), as in '*Stranger Things*', '*The Walking Dead*', '*Saving Private Ryan*' or '*Little Miss Sunshine*'. If we can't identify with the protagonist, we're usually in trouble, see 01 We Don't Care About the Protagonist. We have a main protagonist in many stories, but not all, as explained in 18 There Is No Clear Protagonist. The protagonist can be the *main character* as well, but not necessarily, as mentioned in 28 The Protagonist Is Not Strong Enough. A protagonist isn't the same as a *hero* (conceptually positive character), as detailed in 37 The Protagonist Is a Conventional Hero.

R

Repetitive: See *Episodic*.

Resolution: See *Dramatic Irony*.

Raising the Stakes: See *"What's at Stake?"*

S

Scene: See *Dramatic Scene*.

Second Act: See *Three-Act Structure (dramatic)*, *Three-Act Structure (logistical)* and 07 The Story Sags in the Middle.

Sequence: See *Dramatic Sequence*.

Set-Up: A set-up is the first step in *foreshadowing*, when we plant an element before it pays off later (see *Planting*), and in *dramatic irony*, when we give the audience information that at least one character (the victim) isn't aware of. In comedy, when we set up a gag, we misdirect the audience. Then with a *surprise* we turn the situation around (*pay-off* or punchline). The set-up can also be the *beginning* of the story (first ten to fifteen minutes in a feature film or series first episode / pilot), when we introduce the *characters*, the *story world* and *what's at stake*. See 04 The Story Is Linear, Feels Predictable, 25 The Narrative Is Episodic or Repetitive and 03 The Story Takes Too Long to Start.

Stakes: See "*What's at Stake?*"

Steadfast Character: A character who doesn't change or grow, who remains essentially the same from the beginning until the end of the story, which isn't necessarily a problem, for example in sitcoms. See *Character Evolution* and 05 The Characters Are Flat, Two-Dimensional.

Story Structure: A combination of *plot*, *character* and *theme*, as well as *managing conflict* (Who wants / needs what and why?) and *managing information* (Who knows what when?). Not to be confused with story format. See If You Want to Find Out More... to download a free sampler (first fifty pages) of *Screenwriting Unchained*, as this is developed in the *Introduction* and the first chapter: *The Story-Type Method, a New Framework for Developing Screenplays*. See also 19 The Script Feels Formulaic and 35 The Script Is Unnecessarily Complex.

Story-Type, Story-Type Method: There are three main story-types (according to the Story-Type Method): *plot-led stories*, where the main problem lies outside the protagonist (in antagonistic characters or nature); *character-led stories*, where the main problem lies within the protagonist; *theme-led stories*, where the main problem lies in society and is usually not solvable, which leads to a *multi-stranded narrative*, a collection of storylines exploring the same *theme*. Not all stories have to fit one of the main story-types, which are mostly templates to stimulate creativity. Many stories are *hybrids* or *exceptions*. See 02 We Don't Care About the Story, 19 The Script Feels Formulaic and 35 The Script Is Unnecessarily Complex.

Story World: The story world defines the setting, the environment in which the story takes place. It can be anything from an everyday environment in a contemporary drama, to an entirely invented world in a fantasy or science-fiction story. Whether the story takes place in the real world or in an invented world, the rules of the story world should be consistent and make sense. See 36 The Supernatural Element Is Too Vague.

Strand: Each individual storyline in a *multi-stranded narrative* is a strand. It's similar to a *subplot* in a conventional *narrative*, but as there is no main plot (no main *dramatic action* or *evolution*), there can't be subplots, so they are called strands. In TV Series, strands are called storylines, but it doesn't mean there is no main plot. See 29 The Plot Is Slowed Down By Unconnected Storylines.

Structure: see *Story Structure*.

Subgoal: A way for the *protagonist* to reach the *goal*. It often defines a *dramatic sequence*, which is a succession of scenes connected to the same *dramatic action*. See 25 The Narrative Is Episodic or Repetitive and 07 The Story Sags in the Middle.

Sub-Subgoal: A way for the *protagonist* to reach the *subgoal*. It often defines a dramatic *scene*, which is a succession of beats connected to the same *dramatic action*. See 16 The Scenes Are Aimless, There Is No Dramatic Conflict.

Subplot: A storyline exploring a problem less important than the problem explored in the main plot but connected to it. Usually we don't have more than two or three subplots in a story. Subplots are often used to explore a *theme* (what the story is about). In a *plot-led story*, there is often a *character-led* subplot, a smaller internal problem that the protagonist needs to resolve. This subplot usually defines a need for the protagonist to grow. When there is no main plot, for example in a *multi-stranded narrative*, subplots are called *strands*.

Surprise (or **Twist**): A piece of information that the audience doesn't expect. Surprise is one of the tools linked to *managing information* in a story, along with *mystery*, *dramatic irony* and *suspense*. See 04 The Story Is Linear, Feels Predictable.

Suspense: To generate suspense, the audience needs to know where danger – physical, emotional or psychological – is coming from. Hitchcock, the "Master of Suspense", uses the following situation to explain it: If two characters are talking about the weather, there is no suspense, but if you then show the audience that there is a bomb under the table, suddenly, we want to yell at the characters "Get out!". In this example, Hitchcock uses *dramatic irony* (telling the audience something, in this case about a danger, that at least one character is unaware of) to generate suspense. However, we can have suspense without dramatic irony. As long as the audience knows where the threat comes from, there is suspense, even if all the characters are aware of the danger. Suspense is one of the tools linked to managing information, along with *mystery*, *surprise* and *dramatic irony*. See 04 The Story Is Linear, Feels Predictable and 10 The Ending Doesn't Work.

T

Teaser Flashback: When we need to take some time to introduce our characters or the story world, it might be helpful to start the narrative (film, episode) in the middle or even towards the end of the dramatic action, before going back to the beginning. This teaser could show an exciting event, a conflictual or desperate situation or reveal a puzzling piece of information that will not only grab the attention of the audience but also set up interesting questions, usually using *mystery* or *dramatic irony*. That way, when we go back to the beginning of the story, not only is the audience hooked, but they can watch the unfolding events with the additional knowledge, curiosity or anticipation of conflict to come brought by the teaser. Often used in TV Series, for example in '*The Walking Dead*', '*Breaking Bad*', '*The Queen Gambit*' or '*Occupied*'. Just be careful not to provide an answer to the *dramatic question* in the teaser, as this could undermine the emotional involvement of the audience during the rest of the story. For this reason, if the teaser comes from the end of the story, it's usually a good idea to choose a moment before or during the *climax* ('*Run All Night*') rather than after it ('*John Wick*'). See 01 We Don't Care About the Protagonist, 03 The Story Takes Too Long to Start and 30 The Script Contains Too Much Exposition.

Time-Lock: We have a time-lock when there is a limited amount of time for the *protagonist* to reach a *goal*. This increases the tension and raises the stakes. A classic time-lock is a bomb about to blow-up in an action movie, but you can use more subtle time-locks, for

example if you give your protagonist only *Two Days, One Night* to get her job back, or 24 hours to stop a terrorist plot — each episode showing one hour in real time — in the TV series '*24*'. See 07 The Story Sags in the Middle and 10 The Ending Doesn't Work.
Thematic Acts: See *Theme-Led Story*.
Theme: What the story is about. One of the essential elements of story structure, along with *character* and *plot*. See *Theme-Led Story* below and 39 The Theme Overshadows the Story.
Theme-Led Story: A *multi-stranded narrative* where the main problem usually lies in society. This problem could also be spiritual or philosophical. Often, it can't be resolved. In a theme-ted story, there isn't one *protagonist* over the whole story, as there isn't one *character* – or group of characters – experiencing more conflict than the others. There is no main *plot* as there is no main *dramatic action* or *evolution*. There can't be *subplots* when there is no main plot, so we call each storyline a *strand*. In a theme-led story, we don't have three *dramatic acts* as there is no main dramatic action or evolution, but we have three thematic acts: Act 1, before the audience understands what the theme is; Act 2, while the theme is explored; Act 3, the consequences of this exploration. Examples: '*Crash*', '*Magnolia*', '*Dunkirk*', '*Game of Thrones*', '*Deadwood*', '*Occupied*', '*Big Little Lies*', '*Parenthood*'. Some theme-led stories, such as '*Cloud Atlas*', are also non-linear. See 19 The Script Feels Formulaic, 18 There Is No Clear Protagonist and 39 The Theme Overshadows the Story.
Third Act: See *Three-Act Structure (dramatic)*, *Three-Act Structure (logistical)* and 17 The Script Loses the Plot in the Third Act.
Three-Act Structure (dramatic): A story is structured in three dramatic acts when it's designed around a main *dramatic action* or a main *dramatic evolution*. In this case, we have three *dramatic acts* because we have what happens before the audience understands what the *protagonist* wants or needs (dramatic Act 1); then we have a dramatic Act 2 that shows what happens while the protagonist tries to reach their *goal* (*conscious want* or *unconscious need*). This triggers the *dramatic question*: Will the protagonist reach their goal? Towards the end of this dramatic Act 2, during the *climax*, we provide an answer to this dramatic question: Yes, the protagonist reaches the goal or No, the protagonist fails. After the climax, once the protagonist has succeeded or failed and given up, we enter

dramatic Act 3, which shows the consequences of the dramatic action or evolution in the story world. Before, during and after a main dramatic action or evolution. This is what defines a dramatic three-act structure. These dramatic acts have no fixed lengths, though Act 1 tends to be fairly short (usually around five to fifteen minutes) and Act 3 very short, as once the action or evolution is over we want to go home. Act 2 usually covers most of the story and is divided into *dramatic sequences*, often designed around *subgoals*, which are ways for the protagonist to reach the goal. Not all stories are designed this way, for example *theme-led stories* and *hybrids* or *exceptions* tend to be structured differently, but all stories can use the dramatic three-act structure to design their parts: dramatic acts, sequences, *scenes, subplots, storylines* or *strands*, thanks to the *fractal aspect of story structure*. This is detailed in *Screenwriting Unchained*, using many info-graphs and examples. See also 01 We Don't Care About the Protagonist, 19 The Script Feels Formulaic, 02 We Don't Care About the Story and 16 The Scenes Are Aimless, There Is No Dramatic Conflict.

Three-Act Structure (logistical): A story formatted according to the logistical three-act structure is divided into three acts according to an arbitrary number of pages or minutes. Act I (beginning) covers twenty-five percent of the story, Act II (middle) fifty percent, Act III (end) twenty-five percent. The second act is divided in two equal parts by a *midpoint* in the middle of the story. This division in three logistical acts has no real justification and is about format, not structure. Usually, a dramatic structure can be found underneath if the story is well-designed. For example, a TV movie is formatted in seven logistical acts because of six commercial breaks, but is designed in three dramatic acts. Understanding this difference between logistical and dramatic acts is crucial. I explore this in detail in *Screenwriting Unchained*, using many info-graphs and examples. See   *Three-Act Structure (dramatic) and* 19 The Script Feels Formulaic, 02 We Don't Care About the Story, 03 The Story Takes Too Long to Start, 07 The Story Sags in the Middle and 17 The Script Loses the Plot in the Third Act.

Twist: See *Surprise* and *Encore Twist*.

U

Unconscious Need: When the character needs to change, to move on, we call this their unconscious need. The *conscious want* of a protagonist (goal) defines the *dramatic action*, while the unconscious need defines the *dramatic evolution*. In *character-led stories, what's at stake* is the unconscious need of the protagonist. In *plot-led stories*, it's the conscious want, although there is often an unconscious need as well that defines a *character-led subplot*. See 05 The Characters Are Flat, Two-Dimensional.

V

Villain: Conceptually negative character who opposes a conceptually positive protagonist (*hero*). A Villain isn't the same as an *Antagonist*, and not all stories need a villain. See 26 The Villains or Antagonists Are Weak or Unconvincing and 37 The Protagonist Is a Conventional Hero.

Visual Storytelling: Essential tool used to convey the story visually as opposed to using dialogue (show rather than tell). This can usually be achieved using *foreshadowing*. See 11 The Screenplay Is Written Like a Novel, 31 The Drama / Conflict Is Told But Not Shown and 09 The Screenplay Is Too Dry or Not Visual Enough.

W

"What's at Stake?": The question most often asked by development execs or producers when they don't care about a story. It means "Why should we want to know what's going to happen next?" and if this isn't clear, the story starts with a significant handicap. To identify what's at stake in a story, answer the following question: What will happen if the *protagonist* fails to solve the main problem in the story? Or, more generally, what happens if the main problem in the story isn't solved. Make sure this defines something that makes us feel sad, anxious or terrified, or any negative feeling you can come up with. It should be something that we don't want to see happen to the *characters*. For example, in *'Silver Linings Playbook'*, if Pat doesn't change, he goes back to jail or to psychiatric hospital and he doesn't get to spend the rest of his life with Tiffany. In '*The Walking Dead*', '*Gravity*' or '*Misery*', the protagonist's life is at stake. In the first season of '*Stranger Things*', it's Will Byers' life as well as the Hawkins community as a whole that's at stake. In order to increase or renew the interest of the audience in the story, it can be useful to keep raising the stakes: make it so that the consequences of the protagonist failing get even worse as the story progresses. You can raise the stakes over the whole story, but also over a dramatic sequence or scene, depending on what the *subgoal* or *sub-subgoal* is. See <u>02 We Don't Care About the Story</u>.

If You Want to Find Out More...

We hope you enjoyed reading

THE SCREENWRITER'S TROUBLESHOOTER

To access free content including case studies, interactive story tool, samplers of our books and online training, please register at
www.screenplayunlimited.com/register

To receive an extra 10% OFF our online courses at
www.screenplayunlimited.com/online-courses/
use the discount code **TSTBK10** during checkout

Made in United States
Troutdale, OR
01/25/2024

17163505R00139